Gil Seon-Ju

(1869–1935)

On the Publication of the
Korean Christian Leaders Series

The Korean Christian Church, having experienced phenomenal church growth and a great passion for missions within its short history, is proud of its place as the leading representative of Christianity in Asia. During its brief history, the Korean Church has lived through a great variety of experiences marked by persecution and suffering, zeal and dedication, church growth and foreign missions—a breadth of experience unprecedented in 2000 years of Christianity. These experiences have been conveyed in written works that include debates between Confucian scholars and Catholic converts, as well as meditations, sermons, essays, and poems that elevated persecution and martyrdom to reflections on the next world and true faith.

Through the publication of the Korean Christian Leaders Series, the Korea Institute for Advanced Theological Studies (KIATS) seeks to organize the inheritance of the Korean Christian Church and to share it with Christians around the world. This project will first involve selecting and compiling a body of manuscripts of religious or literary value— manuscripts that clearly present the characteristics of Korean Christianity from its beginnings up to the present. Our primary subject matter includes the writings of church leaders (theologians as well as pastors), and works by social leaders, politicians, thinkers, literary persons, and artists who identified with and served the Korean Church. In organizing and selecting the original manuscripts, we will first work with each author's printed manuscripts, including sermon texts, theses, essays, poems, and written declarations.

The priceless writings of Korean Christian leaders—diverse works that have been buried until now—will become accessible through the publication of this series, which endeavors to re-illuminate the history of Christianity and discover in it the roots of our faith. Through this we will be able to appreciate again the lives and faith of our predecessors who lived and died with passion, as role models of faithful Christians. We will be able to reflect on our own age, and re-envision God's great plan for the future of the Korean Church. Furthermore, this series will allow an appreciation of the characteristic warmth and ingenuity of Korean Christians, and a taste indigenous to Korean faith.

January 2008

Kim Jae-Hyun

Director, The Korea Institute for Advanced Theological Studies

Korean Christian Leaders Series

Gil Seon-Ju

Essential Writings

Selected
by
The Korea Institute for Advanced Theological Studies

The KIATS Press
Seoul, Korea, 2008

Korean Christian Leaders Series

Founded in 2004 for the purpose of 1) cultivating Christian leaders who connect different generations, 2) compiling and globalizing the legacy of Korean Christianity, 3) enabling mutual understanding and communication between Christianity in the East and the West, and 4) creating a trans-denominational space for churches and believers, the Korea Institute for Advanced Theological Studies (KIATS) emphasizes "people, infrastructure, and network."

KIATS seeks those who "steal a glance at the secret of heaven and realize it on earth," and raises them to become people who have the power and vision to undertake research on Christianity with a global perspective. By "offering a place of research for Korean Christianity," KIATS provides Korean Christians with a base and environment for church and theological research; by assisting in the formation of a partner relationship between Asian Christianity and Western Christianity, KIATS stives to be a bridge for mutual benefit.

Publishing Date: January 30, 2008
Published by The KIATS Press, Seoul, Korea
Publishing Director: Jae-Hyun Kim
Translator: Hannah Kim
Cover Design: HONG SUNG SA, Ltd.
ISBN: 978-89-960550-1-3
Printed and bound in Korea

Dedicated to

Song Jae-Sik

"A Walking Lump of Clay"

Senior Pastor of Suhrim Presbyterian Church

Suhrim Presbyterian Church

(Established in 1946, Gwangju, Korea)

The Church that Leads toward the Future:
In a century marked by endless competition and uncertainty,
the Suhrim Church seeks to open the way for human beings
to live humanely,
and aspires to help resolve those impossible dilemmas of life.

CONTENTS

III. The Life of Christians

IV. The Dawn of Peace

Pastor Gil Seon-Ju:
The Cornerstone of the Korean Protestant Church

Min Kyoung-Bae

Chair Professor, Baeseok University

Reverend Yeonggye, Gil Seon-Ju (1869—1935) was Korea's first Protestant pastor and the pioneer of what has become the remarkable phenomenon of Korean Christianity. His faith is the model of the orthodox faith guarded by the Korean Protestant Church today, and his character and integrity have become the standard which today's Korean Christians strive to emulate. What follows points out the place that Reverend Gil Seon-Ju occupies in the history of Korean Protestant Christianity.

Reverend Gil Seon-Ju's Importance in Korean Church History

Reverend Gil Seon-Ju was active from the 1890s to the

1930s, which were the founding years of the Korean Protestant Church. He planted churches throughout the country and helped them develop into the prototypes of today's Korean churches. It is estimated that Reverend Gil delivered more than 17,000 sermons, and that his sermons were heard by over 380,000 people. He planted churches in some 60 locations, and those who entered church leadership or theological studies under his influence numbered in the hundreds. More than 3,000 converts were baptized by Reverend Gil, and the total number of people who were converted to Christianity under his evangelization surpassed 70,000. Moreover, within 35 years, Reverend Gil covered a trail of roughly 10,000 kilometers, crisscrossing the Korean peninsula and traveling as far as Manchuria. In this way he traveled about in Korea and China, leading revival meetings and Bible classes.

Reverend Gil Seon-Ju was one of 33 signers of Korea's Independence Declaration. As this indicates, he was one of several good shepherds who proclaimed the hope and the comfort of a new age to his people in their time of oppression under the Japanese regime. Reverend Gil's convictions about the transformation of the age are also apparent in his exposition, *Malsehak* (*A Study of the End Times*). His lectures on the end times gave hope to a people sunk in despair. At one time he even participated in the Independence League to raise awareness of the future. But he eventually gave up direct involvement in political activities in order to commit himself to evangelism. However, unable to give up his passion for the enlightenment of the masses, he strove to evangelize the workers' union of Pyeongyang, an activity that might be seen as the Korean Church's first venture in evangelizing industrial workers. As a testament to Reverend Gil's passion for education, the neighborhood school that he started in Pandong, Pyeongyang in 1898 grew into the Sungdeok and Sunghyeon Schools.

Reverend Gil Seon-Ju also started the tradition of early morning prayer meetings in 1906, and the practice of praying aloud in one voice was also his idea. He solidified the Korean Church into a church of prayer, and set an example for generations to come by his habit of Bible reading and biblical practice. For instance, it is said that Reverend Gil read through the Old Testament 30 times, the New Testament 100 times, 1 John more than 500 times, and while imprisoned during the March 1st Movement, he read through The Revelation of John 1,200 times. The Bible became like a life force flowing in his body.

The Life of Reverend Gil Seon-Ju

Gil Seon-Ju was born to Gil Bong-Sun on March 25th, 1869 in Anju, South Pyeong'an Province [in what is now North Korea]. The family was relatively well off, and from a young age Gil was able to study the classics. He became famous for his intelligence, and at the age of 12, he wrote a sympathetic poem about a poverty-stricken woman, revealing his literary talent and the wealth of his imagination.

Before embracing Christianity, Gil was deeply engrossed in Seondo [an Eastern mystical practice], and revealed unusual enlightenment and spiritual concentration, remaining in prayer and meditation in the mountains for months at a time. This indicates his deep connection with the roots of his Korean psyche.

One day in 1897, Gil received a copy of John Bunyan's *The Pilgrim's Progress* from the missionary S. A. Moffet, and Kim Jong-Seop, a personal friend who later became a pastor. Upon reading this book he was moved to tears and eventually found rest in the Christian gospel. He was baptized at the age of 29. News of Gil Seon-Ju's conversion found its way into American Sunday School announcements and even into the German Church. Many people were moved by the story and sent donations.

In 1898, at the age of 30 Gil Seon-Ju became the *yeongsu* [a leadership position in a church not yet officially institutionalized] of the Jangdaehyeon Church. As a result, the church grew to 1,000 members. In 1901, at the age of 33 he was elected as an elder of the church. In 1903, Gil was appointed assistant pastor at Jangdaehyeon Church, the largest church in Pyeongyang, as well as assistant itinerant pastor to churches in each region of Hwanghae Province. In the same year he enrolled in the Pyeongyang Presbyterian Seminary and in 1907, became one among seven of Korea's first seminary graduates. In September of 1907, the year of the Great Revival of Pyeongyang, Gil was ordained and was appointed senior pastor of the Jangdaehyeon Church the following month.

The Great Revival of Pyeongyang, the birth of the revival in the Jangdaehyeon Church, and the ordaining of Gil Seon-Ju were pivotal events in the history of the Korean Church. In particular, the Great Revival of Pyeongyang in 1907 was one of the most important events in Korean Church History. Headlines in prominent newspapers all over the world reported the transformation of the Korean Church and the Korean people. With this advent of the Holy Spirit, unceasing praise was poured onto the Korean Church, and it was declared that the Korean Church had emerged to become a proper Christian Church that could teach the churches of the world.

The man called by the Holy Spirit to stand at the forefront of this revival was none other than the Reverend Gil Seon-Ju. Beginning the previous year, he had been leading Bible classes, and one person in Hwanghae Province to be converted through the work of the Holy Spirit during these classes was Kim Ik-Du, who would later become a leading revival preacher. On January 6th, 1907, the fire of the Holy Spirit fell upon the Jangdaehyeon Church. The entire congregation was gathered in a prayer meeting led by Reverend Gil, when everyone was suddenly swept up in the fire of the Holy Spirit. Overcome with contrition, they began confessing their sins, and a movement of repentance unprecedented in the Korean Church took place on the spot. After experiencing such a manifestation of the Holy Spirit, the Korean Church became settled in its identity as "God's Church."

One Sunday in 1908, the Jangdaehyeon Church would witness the baptism of 200 people, and in 1922, membership grew to 1,358. When considering that the population of Pyeongyang at the time was just under 40,000, such growth in membership was remarkable.

But times were changing. The ideologies of communism

and socialism were spreading in Korean society. The youth of the nation raised a banner of opposition against Reverend Gil's conservative faith and in 1926, they even organized a boycott. As a result, Reverend Gil resigned as senior pastor of Jangdaehyeon Church and took on the status of emeritus pastor. But the outcome of this was that he would begin an age of revival in the Korean Church by traveling the country leading revival services.

At the age of 63, Reverend Gil Seon-Ju was appointed temporarily to the Ihyangri Church, founded in 1933. On November 25th, 1935, on the fifth morning of early prayer meetings held during the Pyeongseo Synod Bible Classes at Gochang Church in Gangseo County, Reverend Gil collapsed, falling unconscious. He failed to recover consciousness and was called to the Lord the following day at 9:30 in the morning. His funeral was held by the Pyeongyang Synod in the main auditorium of Soongsil Professional School. Reverend Lee Seung-Gil, head of the Pyeongyang Synod presided, and the sermon was delivered by Reverend Jeong In-Gwa, the general assembly chairman. Reverend Gil's personal history was presented by Reverend Kim Hwa-Sik. More than 5,000 people attended his funeral, attesting to the influence Reverend Gil had extended in the Korean Church.

As we have seen, Reverend Gil Seon-Ju was a cornerstone of the Korean Church. His prior deep involvement in the traditional Korean religious practice of *Seondo* became a significant marker of his having embraced Christianity as an archetypal Korean. In collaboration with Presbyterian missionaries, Reverend Gil founded The Independent Synod, Korea's first synod. He led the great revival movement of 1905–1907, and he set the framework of Korean faith and piety based on the practice of prayer and Scripture reading. He also participated in the founding of the Independence Movement and the labor movement, and brought about a grassroots Christianization of the country through his itinerant Bible classes and revival meetings. He left behind historical works such as *Pyeongyang Sanjeonghyun Gyohoesa* (*A History of the Pyeongyang Sanjeonghyeon Church*) and *Pyeongyang Yeonhab buinhoe Sagi* (*A Historical Record of the Pyeongyang United Women's Association*), and published sermons and writings on preaching. He was truly a leading figure of the first generation of the Korean Protestant Church.

Primary Works

In spite of a busy schedule, Reverend Gil Seon-Ju worked

with unusual energy and left behind many written works, offering a look into his theology and faith. As if reflecting the influence of John Bunyan on his conversion, Reverend Gil used his distinctive approach to *The Pilgrim's Progress* to write *Haetaron* (*Sloth*; The original English title was *Indolence*) and *Mansa Seongchwi* (*The Attainment of All Things*). Many of his sermons and sermon outlines were compiled into *Gangdae Bogam* (*A Pulpit Handbook*), which became the model of outline-based sermon creation for countless Korean pastors. Gil's *Malsehak* (*A Study of the End Times*) which seemed to mirror the darkness of his times, became an important eschatological work in the history of the Korean Protestant Church. *Sallim Cheosa Chunmongga* (*A Song of the Gentleman's Springtime Dream amid the Mountains and Trees*), which depicts Gil's circumstances prior to his conversion, reveals his deep knowledge of classical studies and Eastern philosophy. Other works include *Seonggyeong Yojip* (*A Collection of Bible Essentials*), *Geogeun Jip* (*A Collection of Maxims*), *Joseongwa Judae Pungsog Yugo* (*A Classification of Korean and Jewish Customs*), and *Yehwa Jip* (*A Collection of Parables*).

The Structure of This Volume

This volume is a collection of 28 sermons and important writings that provide a good look into the faith and the life of Reverend Gil Seon-Ju. The content is divided into four parts: Part One consists of sermons based on Reverend Gil's interpretation of the seven sentences spoken by Jesus while hanging on the cross. As if speaking directly to the nation's suffering, he takes the last words spoken by Jesus in his suffering, and with insightful interpretations, turns them into messages of hope and blessing. Part Two features the themes of life, soul, love, and other such central values of the Christian faith presented in Reverend Gil's distinctive and powerful language. Part Three addresses sin, judgment, and the duties of the Christian in colorful illustrations that utilize Chinese characters and idiomatic Korean, conveying the message with a distinctively Korean flavor. Part Four contains lesser-known writings that provide a fuller portrait of Reverend Gil Seon-Ju as preacher and leader of the people. The two pieces that were published in *Christ Newspaper* reveal Reverend Gil's characteristic style of Bible interpretation. Also, "The Meaning of Thanksgiving Day in the Joseon Tradition," shows how Thanksgiving took root in Korea. Unfortunately, "The Book of Peace" was partially lost due to Japanese censorship, but it spoke boldly of peace during a time of violence. *A Pulpit Handbook* shows the prototype of Korean outline-based sermons. *A Commentary on the Book of Daniel*, though short, reveals the significance of the desire for prophecy, vision, and eschatology during the age of Japanese colonization.

The Influence of Reverend Gil Seon-Ju's Works on Later Generations

Reverend Gil Seon-Ju used an unusual method of starting with the foundation of scriptural passages and mixing analogies with semantic interpretations to make Scripture come alive and touch the marrow of the lives of his listeners. He possessed extraordinary powers of observation that allowed him to link the trivial details of daily life to Biblical teachings. There were very few preachers who presented Scripture with such relevance to a person's real-life issues.

Reverend Gil's sermons centered on God's love, the grace of the blood of Christ, and the power of the Holy Spirit. He never departed from that core, and he did not tolerate any diversion from it. Accordingly, his sermons were sometimes frightening in their criticism and admonition. One example is "The Responsibility of the Episcopacy," a sermon contained in this volume which he opens with the apology, "My words will be strong and my examples might be flawed."

Reverend Gil Seon-Ju was one of several figures who laid the foundations of Korean Protestant Christianity. If the Korean Church has become a worldwide church, perhaps the reason lies in the apostolic tradition that started with Reverend Gil's faith, his preaching, and his orthodoxy, standing with unusual strength at such an early time in the history of the Korean Church. He was the greatest pastor and theologian of his time, showing clearly to the Korean people what Christianity is. At the beginning of Korea's modern age, Reverend Gil Seon-Ju showed that the Christian gospel is not merely a matter of heaven after death, but that it has actual relevance to the issues of all people at this very moment. The collection of works in this volume will present a vivid depiction of Reverend Gil Seon-Ju's deep insight and passion.

Explanatory Notes

1. For the sake of retaining the original author's voice, scriptural passages are translated to match closely the wording used by Gil Seon-Ju in the original text.

2. Errors in the author's citation of scriptural passages have been corrected by the editors.

3. Words or phrases in brackets have been added by the editors to clarify meanings in the original text. Also, where a passage requires contextual information, it is marked with an asterix and followed by an editorial explanation.

I. The Lord's Seven Words Spoken from the Cross

"Forgive This Crowd"

Jesus had toiled for 33 years in the human world, and even on the cross where he was being crucified to the very end for the sake of saving humankind from sin he spoke seven times. Perhaps there were those who haphazardly speculated as if it were the truth that, "Since Jesus was God, crucifixion on the cross was not that much of a suffering." But Jesus, while of course being God as the Son of Man, namely, a complete human, received a flesh-ripping punishment. The Lord's suffering was not only a punishment according to the law of Moses but also a type of spiritual punishment as a replacement-death for all the sin of humankind. What the Lord received was such a great spiritual and physical punishment, a great suffering more than the culmination of suffering in hell for all ages that even the universe could not handle it, causing the day's sun to lose its light. Since the earth could not handle it either, there was a suffering so great it could not keep from breaking.

On this cross of suffering, he spoke seven times. He

prayed, told sinners the way, gave his last words to his mother, and sincerely appealed to God. For his enemies, he prayed, "Forgive this crowd"; to the robber, "Surely, today you will be with me in paradise"; looking upon his mother, "Woman, behold your son"; to God, *Eloi Eloi, lama sabachtani*"; and recalling the Scriptures, he said, "I am thirsty"; "Father, into your hands I lift my spirit"; and "It is finished." These are the seven words of the Lord upon the cross, and thus one can say that this is the summary of the gospel and the apex of Christ's mental state. The believer must absolutely know all the holy words of the Lord, but he must especially keep in mind these words to memorialize, believe and follow the Lord's great suffering, his great passion.

The Great Love Proven by Blood

The first word the Lord gave upon the cross is recorded like this in Luke 23:34: "Father! Forgive these people. They do not know what they do." This was the first sound heard after the heavens were made and life was born; the breadth and height of God's manifestation of unlimited love is infinite, and thus it cannot be described by any method. Jesus did not only put into practice while on earth exactly that which he commanded, to love one's enemies and set a precedent, but even on the cross he also personally practiced it and with his great love he marked the command he gave with a seal by the pouring of his blood.

Though it is not that there are no lessons of sacrificing one's body to achieve correct value given by holy men in this world, the reason their lessons do not mount up to Jesus' prayer is the distance. There are patriots who shed their blood for the sake of their country and women who forsake their lives to guard their fidelity, but forgiving my enemies and praying for those who kill me is something that only Jesus did. In the Bible, Stephen, who was the first Christian martyr, followed the Lord's precedent and forgave his murderers and simply prayed for them, too.

The History of Humankind is the Trace of the Blood of Revenge

Under David's command there was a general named Joab who was a brave soldier of a hundred wars and a hundred victories, and a veteran statesman who performed great deeds to help build the nation. According to the record of II Samuel chapters 2 and 3, David's servants and Saul's son Ish-Bosheth's servants were jeering at each other in the region of Gibeon, and eventually a fight broke out between them. As Ish-Boseth's commander Abner could not stop

Joab's third younger brother Asahel from following him, he unavoidably pierced and killed Asahel with the butt of his spear. Even after Abner returned to David, Joab took revenge on Abner and killed him. Joab was a brave warrior but he was a weak man who could not triumph over the desire for revenge in his heart.

What good is it to talk about brave men? Even though David was a rare, wise, virtuous king and a heroic figure, according to the historical account in II Samuel chapter 16, while he was fleeing from Absalom's war he was cursed by Shimei in Bahurim and in that situation he generously showed the tolerance to forgive. But on his deathbed, he gave his dying wish to his son Solomon to kill Shimei for revenge. It is not only that. Even for Joab, whom David considered his hands and feet, David did not let Joab's gray head go down to the grave in peace. When the sage king is like this, what good is it to talk about ordinary people? There is a saying, "Rare is the sage who remains upright when standing before riches." In front of enemies there are no brave warriors, no sage kings, and no benevolent person.

It is said that the history of humankind is the bloodied trail of war, and this is a record of revenge. O Humankind that pass through life leaving a trail of the blood of revenge—if you would bend down before the truth of the cross and reflect upon the pages of human history, it would become clear that the history of mankind is this trail of evil. If you reflect onto your heart the heart of the Lord hanging on the cross, we would say the sky is lower than the heart of Jesus, and our minds are like the grave.

Forgiveness is the Noblest Virtue

Studying the Bible is an important task in the life of faith, but if one faces the Bible with an unflinching heart, how will the Lord's word be made known? Spreading the word is a believer's great duty, but if there is no love in that heart then how will one inspire someone? Prayer is the most necessary thing in a life of faith, but if one does not forgive in his heart then will God listen to that prayer? God, who commanded, "If you are offering your gift at the altar and there remember that you brother has something against you, leave your gift there in front of the altar. First go and be reconciled to your brother; then come and offer your gift" (Matthew 5:23–24), receives the prayer of the one who is at peace. Those who desire to become disciples of the Lord–our Lord who blessed his enemies on the cross–must properly release old grudges; only with the heart of forgiving can people come before the Lord.

It is a joyous thing that recently many large sanctuaries are being built. All kinds of organizations being established is also a celebratory event. However, how deplorable it is if the sound of fighting inside that sanctuary gets louder, or how detestable it is if inside that organization people are jealous of each other and engaging in factional disputes? The attitude that present believers display outwardly has a polite form but the inner heart is not like that. It is a fearsome thing that, many times, even as they laugh they wield a sword in their hearts. Those who have enemies, while they are believers, are scary like a venomous snake. Just as the blood of a prophet flowed in Jerusalem, in the church there are acts that cause innocent people to stumble. While they consider themselves righteous, with self-serving hearts they condemn other people as unrighteous. And there are many who are stubborn, asking, "How can I forgive an unrighteous person?" Let's yield one step and say that the other person is unrighteous. Because he is an unrighteous person there is something to forgive; there is nothing to forgive in one who is righteous. Doesn't one forgive because the other has done something wrong?

The heart of enmity is hell. Not forgiving others is not enjoying the joy a believer's heart should rightfully have inside. The heart of forgiveness is heaven. To this person, the Lord unceasingly provides spiritual joy and fills him. Even on the mound of stones that hit and killed him, Stephen's spiritual joy overflowed and he shined like an angel, and heaven opened its gates to him. The religion of Jesus is the religion of forgiveness. Forgiving and forgiving again seventy-seven times was Jesus' life, his lesson, and cross. People of Jesus! Hear this, for it is a sound that the one who forgives others can hear, the voice of the Lord who said on the cross as he shed his blood, "Father, forgive this crowd."

"You Will Be with Me in Paradise"

Luke recorded in his Gospel in chapter 23 verses 39 to 43 the story of one robber who had received the same punishment with Jesus, repenting. Among the two robbers who had received the same sentence, one person slandered Jesus and ridiculed him, but the other repented saying that the punishment they received was befitting of their sin and that Jesus had done nothing wrong, and he became a witness to Jesus' righteousness and believed in him. What's more, he requested, "Remember me when you come into your kingdom." Jesus said to this robber, "I tell you the truth, today you will be with me in paradise," and this was the second thing he said on the cross.

It is easy for people who entered the church a long time ago to think of this word as ordinary. But the true heart of the Lord, who relayed his gospel even in the midst of the greatest pain on the cross, and the love of the Lord, who looked mercifully onto an evil sinner like the robber, are so great and wide that they cannot compare to anything else to such an extent that it would be difficult even to explain.

Also, regarding the robber's salvation it is easy to assume that he did not have the qualifications to be a believer. But even though the time was short, he fulfilled his qualification as a believer. Of course, salvation is grace received without price but in receiving grace one must absolutely meet five conditions, and he possessed these five rules.

First is repentance. Without a doubt, the first thing to do for faith to receive salvation is repentance. This robber first sincerely repented his wickedness. "What we are receiving is fitting for what we have done" are words that he cried out in grievance and repentance; his conscience was ripped just like his flesh ripped by the nails of the cross. Fresh blood flows from his hands and feet and contrition that he cannot bear arises within his heart. There are times when humans repent of their own mistakes and faults and rebuke themselves in the midst of hardship. But if suffering is severe it is rather that wickedness also becomes severe, thus it was with the example of the other robber. Hence, restoring the essence of his conscience in the midst of that extreme pain was not such an easy thing to do. Any one of us will have to immediately repent, acknowledging that what we receive is befitting to our actions. So even if we receive death and hell, we were once sinners with no choice but to say, "It is appropriate for my actions."

The second requirement is to have faith. He fully accomplished the second most precious thing to do as a believer, which is confessing that Jesus is God. That robber, in rebuking the other sinner said, "Do you not fear God?" One can say these words referred to God the Father but it was a reprimand of the sinner's words slandering Jesus, namely the Son, so the "God" in the statement is correctly assumed as referring to the Son. Therefore, he confesses that Jesus is the Son of God. It is rather easy to confess that Jesus is God after seeing him exercise power and authority or seeing the glorified Jesus who is transfigured on the holy mountain, or hearing the voice from heaven saying, "This is my Son, whom I love." But it would be very hard to see Jesus, seized and judged as a sinner like him, as God. It was easy to believe Jesus to be the Messiah when he was being followed by throngs and being lauded Hosanna by the masses. But to believe and follow Jesus as the Messiah when he is being ridiculed by people and when his breath is about to be cut off on the cross is not an easy thing to do. However, that robber believed. His confession of faith, that the Nazarene Jesus who was killed powerlessly is God, is great! Who can say that his faith does not compare to Peter's?

The third is bearing witness to Jesus. The third thing to do

as a believer is to bear witness to Jesus. Giving his last ounce
of strength, the robber testified to Jesus' righteousness
saying, "There is nothing this man has done wrong." Why
couldn't the beloved disciple John, who was loved and
embraced in Jesus' bosom, speak for Jesus in saying that he
had no sin to die on the cross? The head disciple Peter
couldn't testify that Jesus had done nothing wrong but
instead denied him, and the only person who testified that
Jesus was a righteous person was the robber. The disciples
and followers who saw Jesus help the poor people and heal
the sick said, "Jesus is righteous," but as Jesus was on the
cross and about to lose his breath like a sinner, they kept
their mouths closed. When the Lord had given sermons on
righteousness and warned against unrighteousness, those
followers had said, "Yes, that's right," but in the end had all
run away. But how precious is it that he, who had been a
robber in the past, pointed to Jesus and testified that he had
done nothing wrong? The religious figures and masses of
Israel referred to Moses' law that said Jesus was to be killed
and they crucified him on the cross, and even Roman law
sentenced him to death. But the person who denied all this
and spoke and testified for Jesus was this robber, who said,
"There is nothing this man has done wrong." He believed in
the righteousness of the Lord and wanted to receive

salvation, so Jesus also looked upon him as righteous. Who will point to him and call him a thief, or pointing to his confession of faith and testimony say it was not at to the level of Paul's gospel of justification, or not as good as Paul's testimony?

The fourth, hope. The fourth thing to have as a believer is hope. The robber of the past was born again on the cross and said to Jesus, "Jesus, remember me when you come into your kingdom," and he did not lose that eternal hope. He believed in the eternal life after death and Jesus' second coming, and this was the greatest hope for which he earnestly waited. In life, for the most part, it is easy to grow desperate or be discouraged and disappointed in the midst of extreme pain and great sin, but even in the midst of absolute pain he had hope in the future. Even as he confronted immediate death, he eagerly sought the eternal life that was coming; no matter what great sin he had committed in the past, he believed and was hopeful that if he received forgiveness from Jesus he would be a child and citizen of heaven. If the disciples, who often heard Jesus prophesying of his return, had such great hope and belief in his second coming, then the robber's faith was superior. For having seen that Jesus dying with him, he nonetheless hoped for his coming kingdom. His faith was more noble indeed. If the disciples had such great faith and made such great proclamations out of their certain hope of resurrection because they had met the resurrected Jesus, then one cannot say that the faith and the hope of the robber, who saw Jesus dying on the cross yet still sought eternal life from him, was not truly great.

The fifth, prayer. A believer needs to repent, have faith, be a witness, and have hope. And the fifth thing to do is to pray. The previous robber gave the very last moment of his life and strength, and he prayed to Jesus with the last drops of his blood falling, "Jesus! Remember me when you come into your kingdom." "Jesus... Remember me!" What a beautiful and sincere prayer! In every situation in life we should pray, "Jesus! Remember me," and even at one's last breath of life, one should pray, "Jesus! Remember me." With that prayer, one's entire life would be complete.

Conclusion

Jesus, who came to call sinners and find lost sheep, endeavored to find one lost soul even at the most pressing time, to give him the blessings of salvation and eternal life. Therefore, the robber was the last disciple of Jesus. The Lord who lost Judas Iscariot gained this man, and through him the Lord once again saw the joy of finding the one lost sheep among the masses of sheep. Therefore, Jesus gave the greatest approval and mercy to him who was his last disciple, saying, "I tell you the truth, today you will be with me in paradise."

"Woman, Behold Your Son"

The Mother Weeping at the Cross

According to the Gospel of John 19:25–26, the Lord's mother and many female disciples were standing at the cross while Jesus was being crucified. This would have been one of the most terrible and wretched scenes that ever appeared on earth. A beloved child bleeding upon the cross! Beneath the cross, a mother weeping! If human sorrow reached this point, it would be the extreme of extremes; for the world's pain to reach this point would be the agony of agonies.

The heart of the mother standing beneath the cross and staring at the Son of Man bleeding upon the cross is the deep sadness that Simeon prophesied: "One day a sword will pierce your soul" (Luke 2:35). The heart of Jesus on the cross looking down upon his mother crying beneath the cross must have hurt as much as his palms tearing from the iron nail. The Son of Man sent one word in his final moment to his earthly mother, along with the drops of blood falling to the ground: "Woman! Behold your son."

In terms of human feelings, these were words of terrible tragedy, but more than tragedy, these were the greatest words of comfort; in terms of ethics and virtue, these were words of great filial piety fulfilling a son's duty; in terms of providence, it was the great work of redemption.

Commentary on Two Questions

There are two points at issue about these words of Jesus. The first is why did Jesus not refer to his mother as "Mother," but "Woman," and there are some who ask, "Isn't saying 'Woman!' disrespectful?" "Woman" is an expression that is recorded in the Gospel of John chapter 2 verse 4 at the aforementioned wedding banquet in Cana, and it is used two times up to this passage. This was a respectful word people in the past often used to refer to a noblewoman; it is not something that ever suggested contempt or disrespect. It is said that even Saint Augustine used this word to refer to Cleopatra. Hence, the Lord also used this word as a term of reverence. Also, there were reasons why he called her by another respectful word and not "mother." The thirty years Jesus filially served his mother in his family was the time of fulfilling his duty as a human, but upon entering his three-year public life, he no longer was a person who belonged to one family, but he was the Lord of heaven, and on the cross, he was even more so. He called her woman because it was more a relationship of a master and servant, a relationship of the Savior Jesus to Saint Mary, rather than a relationship of mother and son, with Jesus as the son of Mary. And by doing so he also confirmed the title "seed of woman" (Genesis 3:15).

Second, there are some who criticize and ask, "Saint Mary had other real sons like James and Judas, but why did he entrust John with serving his mother?" This does not serve as evidence that Mary had no other children besides Jesus nor does it substantiate the Roman Catholic Church's claim that Mary is the eternal virgin mother. A Bible teacher of a certain church school wrote in a certain theological magazine a few years ago that Jesus entrusted John with serving his mother for the sake of bread and said such and such about financial problems in Christianity, but this is not only such a divergent view distorting the Lord's sacred will and the truth, but also, in the Joseon Church, there are many such lamentable assertions of mistaken doctrine or theories claiming to be true. Even Confucius taught that generally, a dutiful service to one's parents is not only being pious to serve parents' physical needs, but it is also in calming their hearts and minds to make them happy. Christ's sacred will was to correctly guide the faith of his mother Mary.

At this time, Jesus' younger siblings did not even come to the site, and even if they did come, they would have come at a time when they had not yet entered the faith regarding the gospel. Since the beliefs were different, it is unknown whether they would have been able to filially serve her physically, nor could they put their mother's heart and mind at rest, thus there would have been no benefit to her faith, only damage. Therefore, Jesus entrusted his mother to his beloved disciple John saying, "Behold, here is your mother," and accomplished his duty as a son and as the Lord; can there be anything more perfect than this?

Christianity and Filial Piety

A certain Confucian scholar told me, "There is the utmost worship of Heaven in Christianity, but it falls short in dutifully serving one's parents." This was not only a question that the Confucian scholar asked, but there are people in the church who also think this way, and they are mistaken if they say there are many who neglect to be filial to their parents. Generally speaking, Confucianism is a religion of morality that places filial piety at its foundation, and the foundation of the morality of human principle starts at filial piety. However, as our Christianity is a religion that is centered on God, the morality between God and man—loving God with all your heart, soul, and mind—is its foundation, and the morality of love between humans is at the end. Hence, Confucianism and human virtue have their foundation in filial piety, but Christianity's Ten Commandments keep the Commandments One, Two, Three, and Four as the primary commandments to revere God, and from Commandment Five it teaches morality between humans; the Ten Commandments place filial piety as the first of morality between humans.

Therefore, speaking first of filial piety from the standard of so-called worldly morality is losing the foundation. The Christian ethic of serving God and being filial to one's parents is perfect from beginning to end. Then, as a Christian who loves God, there should be no one who does not exercise filial piety and it is difficult to call someone who does not exercise filial piety a Christian. Sincere filial piety is not only performing the three-year mourning in Confucianism [The ritual of wearing mourning clothes for three years after the death of a parent], or watching over the parents' grave, but as it is written in the Ten Commandments of Christianity, filial piety is the foundation of the second commandment—the morality of "loving the neighbor as myself." A person who cannot love his parents who are closest to him cannot love others. Thus someone who is not filial has already violated the commandment to love people. He who has violated this second set of commandments cannot say that he loves God according to the first set of commandments.

As such, filial piety is a precious notion for Christianity. But among young adult believers, occasionally there are those who take after the Westerners and emphasize the love between man and woman and they do not love their parents, thereby committing the sin of being undutiful. This is a tremendous mistake. People like this must be inspired by our Lord's great filial piety and repent. As I get older it is hard for me as well to suppress the grief and regret of not fulfilling my filial duty. Like the lamentation of people of the past, "A tree tries to be still but the wind does not stop," and, "Children try to piously serve their parents but they are already gone," I learned filial piety from Jesus, but my parents are no longer here, so I only have regret and grief. Young men and women, you must not lose your chance, but you must diligently endeavor to obey your parents so you will have no regrets.

Jesus lived at home for thirty years and during eighteen of these years—from the age of twelve to thirty—he obeyed his mother and served her with sweat and toil. It was only after that time of filial service that he left home for a mere three years to do the work of heaven. Having completed the great work of salvation, and even in the midst of extreme hardship, he fulfilled his filial duty to his mother. Who can point to Christianity and say that it lacks the lessons of filial piety, when Jesus fulfilled with his own blood his duty of loving his parent? What kind of believer neglects filial piety even as he follows the cross? I hope that young believers especially make a resolution regarding this.

On the cross, Jesus prayed a great prayer of immense love and mercy for the crowd and opened the way of life for all people of all generations. To the robber, he proclaimed the great will of virtue, opening the door of paradise to the most wicked sinner. Now to his mother, even though he was the Savior, he still regarded as important his duty as a son and he showed all generations the great law of morality: "Parents love your children affectionately, and children be filial to your parents," thereby giving us the standard that our lives should follow.

"Eloi Eloi, Lama Sabachtani"

The Lord Who was Forsaken by People and by the Father

On the cross, Jesus lifted up to God the Father a prayer requesting forgiveness for the unrighteous and incomparably atrocious people. He permitted the salvation of paradise to the utmost wicked robber and fulfilled his duty as a son to his mother and comforted her. These are the three great loves he performed for people. The three great works of forgiveness, salvation, and filial piety were the epitome of his entire life's mission on the cross.

When he looked down on the world from the cross, there were thousands and tens of thousands of people, all sinners. When he looked around to the side there were the outlaws, and in the area close to the cross there stood female disciples and his weeping mother. Looking to the people to the left and right and beneath the cross, the Lord tried to finish the work he had started. Now there was something left to do regarding his relationship with the Father. Thus, he took the place of the sinners below the cross and faced God who remained above the cross.

Jesus' breathing grew agonized, his chest heated up like a furnace, and his holy body was worn down and about to give out. As he stretched his body, the place where the nail had been driven into ached all the more, and as the strength in his muscles gave way, the wounds of his hands and feet ripped more. Thirst arising because of the heat of his body, his heart engorged with blood, his arteries hardening, his muscles stiffening, the pain and dizziness in his head, and so forth, is truly difficult to imagine. The blood flowing from the four wounded places stained the nail heads and whenever the body convulsed, fresh blood spurted and flowed down the pillar of the cross and fell upon the ground. The Lord's pain increased intensely moment by moment, and he was bearing the unbearable suffering of the last moment. But more agonizing was the fact that everyone had completely forsaken him.

Now who were the people remaining around him? The arrogant and vicious priests walking around flapping their holy garments and scholars who lied and thought about ostentation. The deceitful mobs who buy and sell a poor man's hard-toiled labor, maiden's beauty, and slaves' sweat. The reckless rioters and the brutal Roman soldiers encircled him to curse and ridicule him. Aside from the few women, those who had been healed or fed by Jesus, the poor who had been loved by him, the children who had been blessed, and even the crowd of disciples who had learned from him for three years and been loved, had all forsaken him and left.

But even though a great number of people had harmed him, and tens of millions of people forsook him, if only God was with him then what affliction could he feel? If the Lord who had said "Even if you leave me alone, I am not alone, for the Father is with me" (John 16:32) was now being forsaken even by his Heavenly Father, how severe must that agony be! When the Son of God's extreme pain and agony reached this point, the sun in broad daylight could not help but lose its light and the entire earth was covered in darkness. At this, the Lord cried out in a loud voice, *"Eloi! Eloi! Lama sabachtani!"*

Poetry and Prophesy

Eloi Eloi lama sabachtani was in Aramaic, recorded exactly as the Lord said, and it displays the loudest, most intense and deepest shout of exclamation. It was the fourth of the seven words said upon the cross, namely, the central word. This is Psalm 22:1, and it is the prayer of petition of the righteous and holy believer when he meets hardship;

Psalm 71:10–12 and Psalm 69 are in accord with each other in order to prophesy the Messiah's crucifixion. There are four principles in these words. First, there is of course no bitter feeling or criticism; this is a song of the most severe pain, and a prayer of absolute tragedy. When the believers are in sorrow and grievance in the midst of severe adversity, we experience the sadness that comes from feeling as if God is forsaking and leaving us. Jesus, who was the most holy and great priest, is able to understand and take pity on our weak nature and shortcomings through this. The two words, "*Eloi! Eloi*" show that Jesus never lost the will to trust God the Father.

Second, these words fulfill the prophecy of the prophets concerning him.

Third, these words express the severity of the affliction; the mental anguish reached the state more severe than the physical pain. Salmont [an old commentator; difficult to identify] once said, "This is the shriek of a person who temporarily lost the way to commune with God. Fervently seeking faith and relying on God in the midst of darkness, he was troubled by this unprecedented experience, and so one could say this was a shout that was aware of innocence. Therefore, he temporarily lost the joy of fellowship, and this could be a shout because of a severed conversation with the Father.

Indeed, this is a record of the serious experience of being unable to reach deep inside, namely, something that can be experienced only by one who is in a special relationship with us concerning humans, sin, and God's grace." Even without borrowing Salmont's words, we believers are able to see that this is Jesus' suffering. I think even for the author of Psalm 22, it would have been difficult for that expression's spiritual imagination to steal a glance deep inside the Lord's suffering.

Taking the Place of Universal Death and the Sin of Humankind

Fourth, the meaning of these words manifests the duty of atonement that instead took on the sinner's punishment, pain, and death. Some Christian scholars, like Russia's Tolstoy and others who studied Christian documents that did not include the faith of atonement, said that in Jesus' entire lifetime he was consistently brave from beginning to end, but that the one phrase of *Eloi Eloi lama sabachtani* on the cross betrayed his weakness and disappointment. People who are ignorant of the experience of atonement will speak like that. The seventy-year-old Socrates drank poison in the last moment, but instead stayed calm and quiet, and Danjong's [Joseon king of the fifteenth century, 1441–1457] minister Seong Sam-Mun [a civil minister of King Sejong of Joseon, 1418–1456] died burned at the stake, but his chivalric spirit was all the more vivid. Many martyrs were also usually bold at their death, so they say that Jesus' grief and lamentation on the cross was a weakness. However, people saw the death of righteous men and patriots, and they do not know the Savior's death for the sake of another; thus they impudently started an ignorant criticism.

Jesus' death was not a death of one individual but the total pain of experiencing the death of all generations and all sinners, the death of all humanity; by enduring the death of countless people in one body, it was a universal death that took the place of all the forces of death. Also, the holy son Jesus was tempted, and even though he was without sin, still took charge of everybody's sin; when he took the place of the actual sinner, he suffered the pain instead. When we believers become neighbors with people who do not fulfill the duties befitting a person and go against the natural order, we come to feel the pain in our bodies from their wickedness. If that is so, then how much would Jesus' pain, which took on all that wickedness have been?

Once I received a letter saying that a young man started an anti-Christian movement, damaging a sanctuary on Christmas and harming a child, and it made me shake in fear. Because that young man was someone who had been educated by me, the wicked acts that the young man carried out made me afraid and tremble from the thoughts that this was the result of incorrect education and that I might be responsible. When children sin, people experience a heavy pain arising from the sense of responsibility that it was in fact their sin. Jesus' atonement of sin does not stop at feeling the sense of responsibility we experience; he has truly taken charge of the sin and punishment. Just as a carrier's entire toil is delivered to my body, Jesus' assumption of humankind's sin is not a conceptual action in the mind nor is it only legal reasoning; that heavy load of sin is, in reality, delivered to Jesus. This is completely different from the meaning of forgiving the adulterous woman, for he himself took on that filthy sin and punishment on his body and was absolved afterwards. Saying, "Your sins are forgiven, take up your mat and return," is easy for anyone to say, but Jesus took on that sin and said, "Be at peace."

Did Jesus pray a prayer of forgiveness on the cross for the sake of numerous enemies? Did he take on the sin of blasphemy of his wicked and unrighteous enemies, and pray to God to allow the wicked robber to enter paradise? Then these were words that assumed the wretched sin and the punishment of the robber and allowed it to be passed over to his cross. Therefore, Jesus who died on the cross was not a holy person, but the actual sinner, who took on the sins of the enemies who were killing the Son of God. He was in the actual state of being a robber because of the hand-over of the robber's sin. Therefore, Paul taught in his epistle to the Romans, "He sent his son in the form of flesh having sin and resolved sin in the flesh for our sins," and Jesus himself declared his desire, saying, "The Son of Man ... will give his life for many in order to atone for sin" (Matthew 20:28).

Not even the gravitational power of the universe could handle the total weight of the evil committed by all the generations. Even the destructive fire of hell would not be enough for the total punishment of the sin of all generations, but Jesus on the cross carried the entire reality of this sin on his body, and the great pain of that is incomprehensible to a human brain. The God who does not tolerate adulterous women and robbers and forsakes murderers and blasphemers had no choice but to forsake Jesus, who was the reality of all this sin; thus Jesus was forsaken by the Father and had no choice but to shout, "*Eloi Eloi lama sabachtani.*" Jesus carried the totality of death and the total weight of sin on the cross, and through that universal pain of being forsaken by God due to death and sin, he uttered the song and prayer of great shout and lamentation, *"Eloi Eloi lama sabachtani."*

When Jesus cried *Eloi Eloi* with the weight of universal death on his shoulders, its sound went up to heaven and penetrated it while Jesus' blood fell on the earth! Not even the ground could endure it; the earth's core shook so the earth moved and caused an earthquake. The cry of *"lama sabachtani"* that took the place of all humankind's sin shook the entire universe! Hundreds of millions of stars in the galaxy could not help but lose their light! The daylight sun became dark. Oh! *"Eloi Eloi lama sabachtani!"*

"I Am Thirsty"

When Jesus bore the great sin of mankind and fulfilled the great work of redemption, which made him taste the extraordinary spiritual suffering as if he were being abandoned by the Father to the point of crying out, "*Eloi Eloi lama sabachtani,*" the sky and sun lost its light and the earth became dark from twelve to three in the afternoon. At around three in the afternoon, he realized that he had finished the commission God had given him and said, "I am thirsty." He had not been able to feel the physical pain while he was experiencing the fearsome spiritual pain, but as the spiritual pain ceased, he suddenly felt the physical pain as well. Usually, a person nailed to the cross develops an intense fever, and it is said that the throat drying up is an extraordinary pain. Therefore, a soldier who had been guarding Jesus dipped a sponge in vinegar with sympathy and, tying it to hyssop, put it to his mouth. The hyssop is two *cheok* [A *cheok* is normally 30.3 cm] with leaves that are not that long. The cross Jesus was hanging on was not that high, either. The vinegar was actually wine that tasted like vinegar, and it was an inferior drink, the cheapest. Therefore, making him drink vinegar also served as a sign of contempt (Psalm 69:21).

He fulfilled the prophecy of the crucifixion: "They gave me a wineskin to eat and when I was thirsty vinegar to drink." In Matthew 27:34 it says, "There they offered Jesus wine to drink, mixed with gall; but after tasting it, he refused to drink it." Since making him drink wine that tasted like vinegar mixed with gall was an effort to have him forget the pain of the cross, Jesus did not drink it in order not to avoid the pain and feel the full sensation of being crucified.

Normally, one doesn't think that thirstiness is that great a pain. But after bleeding and generating heat, pain that comes from being thirsty is tremendous. It is said that the loudest cry heard on the battlefield is a soldiers' shout of "I am thirsty." A few years ago, I had a serious surgery and couldn't drink water and experienced the dreaded pain that comes from thirst. At that time I remembered the Lord's thirstiness. The Lord took our place when our throats like open tombs would have had to deal with the pain of thirstiness, and the Lord took our place when our tomb-like intestines would have had to be burned in the pain of thirstiness.

Until Jesus suffered on the cross, there were twelve great

physical pains: the first was the blood and sweat he shed on Gethsemane. Having blood and sweat pour out from the pores—there is no other pain like this in history. The second was being unable to sleep, and the third was being bound. The fourth was being whipped; the Lord's holy body was wounded by the tip of a whip, here and there. The fifth was being tried five times in a row: the great strain of being tried five times in twelve hours by Annas, Caiaphas, Pilate, Herod, and Pilate. From what I have experienced in prison, one of the greatest pains is being tried in a court of law. The sixth was wearing the crown of thorns, and the seventh was being ridiculed. The eighth was taking up his cross and going up to Golgotha; Jesus was so afflicted, he fell. The ninth was being stripped of his clothes, and the tenth was being hung on the cross. The eleventh was being thirsty, and the twelfth was tasting the bitter wine.

Is not life so comfortable for the modern believer? Remember. In redeeming us, the Lord experienced extraordinary physical pain—and of course the spiritual pain. "I am thirsty!" This is the last word about the numerous sufferings that the Lord experienced. The Lord allowed us to forever drink the water of life by being thirsty himself.

"It is Finished"

Jesus endured the utmost pain on the cross and declared, "It is finished." This is the completion of human salvation, the universe, and love. In the beginning when God created the heavens and earth and formed all creatures, human life was the greatest manifestation of the universe. However, humanity is incomplete while it is under the authority of sin, Satan, and death; if humanity is incomplete, then the universe is not yet complete.

Now, since the Lord completed the great salvation of humanity through the cross, the universe is complete, and with the completion of salvation and the universe, God's love becomes complete. We see the cross and see the center of the universe, believe the cross and gain the sure effect of salvation, and we see the cross and see the zenith of love. Everything that existed before the cross advanced towards the cross, and everything that appeared after the cross started and advanced anew from the cross; from alpha to the cross, and the cross to omega.

The center of everything is the cross, the center of alpha and omega is the cross, the completion of everything is the cross, and even the completion of alpha and omega is the cross. "It is all finished." The universe, salvation, and love—it is all finished. Everything of everything is all finished.

"Father! Into Your Hands I Commit My Spirit"

The prophecy that reads "Jehovah, God of truth! You have redeemed me and I commit my spirit into your hands" (Psalm 31:5) was fulfilled by the Lord's sacred words he spoke at the very end.

There are people who, pointing out that Jesus committed his spirit, claim the theory of Jesus being a pure man, and they say that his soul is the same as our human souls. But these people are making a serious mistake. While Jesus was a perfect human being with flesh and soul, he is the Lord with perfect Godhood. He was crucified as a human and he commits his soul to the Heavenly Father as a man. Humans created in the image of God sinned, thus only God could forgive the sins, and since humans sinned, only the Son of Man can atone for the sins.

The blood of the Jews and Gentiles was in Adam, and he possessed both male and female. Then, just as the first Adam was the origin of man and woman and the originator of the Jews and Gentiles, the second Adam, Jesus, is the savior of the Gentiles and Jews because in his bloodline he had Gentile grandmothers such as Ruth and Rahab. Jesus was a pure human who did not bear children. Thus Jesus is one who possessed both male and female sexes. Therefore, it is befitting for him to be the savior of men and women. Jesus, who is the savior of the Gentiles and Jews, man and woman, namely, all of humankind, committed his spirit into the Father's hands as a complete human [This phrase that says Adam and Jesus possessed both male and female sexes may arouse a debate of criticism. However, this phrase emphasizes that, as Adam was the origin of the humanity, which includes man and woman, Jesus is the savior of everyone, including the Gentiles, Jews, and man and woman].

The Lord completed his final end as a human being with the seven sacred words, "Father, forgive them"; "Today you will be with me in paradise"; "Woman, behold your son"; "*Eloi Eloi lama sabachtani*"; "I am thirsty"; "It is finished"; and "Father, into your hands I commit my spirit." The Son of Man died. He completed the pain of death on the cross just as people wanted, as he planned, and as the Father allowed. Jesus atoned for all sinners until his very end and then died. Brothers and sisters, look up to the cross and yearn, lend your ears and listen to the Lord's seven words. This is the cry of liberation, the gospel of salvation, the proclamation of victory, and the declaration of completion.

II. Value and Love

The Most Precious Life
John 17:3

The fact that all animals cherish life and detest death is their inborn character of nature and instinct of life in this vast and boundless universe. Therefore, all animals that possess life feel joyful about living and dismal about death. Now, I would like to explain life in three major ways.

The Value of Life

1. Life puts the world at awe

A few years ago, I visited the house of a church member who manages a commercial business. As soon as I arrived at the doorway of the store, I heard the loud sound of laughter. When I entered the store, five to six salesmen were sitting around and laughing loudly as they shared their stories. When I asked what was so funny, one of them pointed to the person sitting next to him and said, "While this person was conducting his business during the last few days, he purchased and sold a certain item, but ended up losing some tens of thousands of *won*. But in this process, there was a

ridiculous incident, and that's why we are laughing like this."
The person who lost tens of thousands of *won* had no sign of
worry on his face either, and was laughing loudly. I thought
to myself, I don't know what items he had bought and how
he had sold them, or what funny incident is hidden
underneath, but how can they be talking so harmoniously in
spite of losing such an enormous amount of money that was
worth at least tens of thousands of *won*? Is the value of
money that worthless?"

When I left that place, I went to an upper street and
arrived at the entrance of another neighborhood. A group of
at least thiry or forty people were standing around, frowning
and shaking their heads; it seemed as if they were turning
pale with astonishment. I considered this odd and asked if
there was some big, shocking incident. One of them took my
wrist and dragged me in the direction of the electric train rail
track. Just as I got to that side, the smell of human blood
pierced my nostrils and I saw that the blood of this person
had drenched the rail and the ground. I was greatly shocked
and asked what had happened. He replied, "A laborer was so
drunk he crossed the track when the train was passing. He
got hit by the train—his entire body was injured and that is
why he bled like this. It is most likely that he is dead."

At that time I wholeheartedly felt the preciousness of

human life. A little earlier, even though it was tens of thousands of won, money that everyone considers most precious, had been lost, people made it out to a trivial chatter and laughter; but now, thirty or forty people were grief-stricken and full of sorrow because of the laborer's death. The value of life seemed enough to move the whole earth. Not only the universe, but it had the power to shock all the heavens and earth.

About twenty years ago during the period of the Great War [World War I, 1914–1918] in Europe, tens of billions of *won* worth of assets were turned into gun smoke and thrown into the sea. As a result, the world suffered a financial panic and all of humankind struggled to live. Surely, this was a significant incident but I do not think it has the value capable of stupefying the people in the world. On the other hand, no one would be shocked to learn that Europe's mountains and rivers were stained with the blood of twenty-five million people at the time of the Great War. If tens of thousands of angels and God in heaven look down on this land of Europe, I am certain they would have been tremendously shocked. This is not my personal theory. It is written in Luke 15:7 that, "there will be more rejoicing in heaven over one sinner who repents than over ninety-nine righteous persons who do not need to repent." How, then, can God in heaven see the bloodshed of twenty-five million, and not be shocked?

2. Life has absolute value

Our Lord demonstrated that the value of one person's life transcends that of the entire world. His word, "What good is it for a man to gain the whole world, yet forfeit his soul?" (Mark 8:36), means that even if one gains this entire world, it is not worth his life.

3. Life holds the highest standing

A proverb of Joseon [the last kingdom of Korea] says, "A dead prime minister is not as good as a living dog" which means even the prime minister does not possess value when he is dead, and even the dog possesses value when he has life.

Today, the reason this world is competing over gold is for the sake of this life; competing for power or economy, competing for science or knowledge, and competing for the army or the navy—all is for this life. Even cultivating morals, sweating, and tasting hardship are for this life; even a certain ethnic group's establishment of a country and expansion of its territorial domain are their attempts to preserve their own nation's life; expansion of air force in each country, production of submarines, construction of steel cannons, and invention of lethal rays are all attempts that harm the enemy's life to preserve their own nation's life. Taking the life away from A is to preserve the life of B, and the sacrifice of the life of B is an attempt to save the life of A. For instance, the reason for destroying the life of livestock is for me to eat that flesh and to preserve my life. Christ shed his blood on the cross and sacrificed his own life to save the lives of all the people of the world. What is most magnificent is the power of life, and what is most precious is also life.

The Source of Life

There is only one source of life. It says in John 17:3, "Now this is eternal life: that they may know you, the only true God, and Jesus Christ, whom you sent," and Colossians 3:3, "For you died, and your life is now hidden with Christ in God." The source of life, then, is God himself. If a person went to a riverside, threw a net and sat there waiting and a certain passerby asked him, "What are you doing, throwing your net and sitting there waiting?" to which he replied, "I threw the net into the river and am sitting here waiting for an apple to get caught in my net." The passerby would think that person was mentally ill. Also, if I went to an apple tree and said I was getting a carp, people would acknowledge me as someone who is mentally ill. If you want to get an apple,

you must go to an apple tree to find it, and if you want to get
a carp, shouldn't you throw a fishing hook or a net into the
river to get it? Just like this, if you want to seek life, you must
seek God, who is the source of life.

Several years ago, there was a time when I was greatly
surprised while reading page 2 of *The Dong-ah Ilbo* [*The
Dong-ah Il-bo* is a Korean daily newspaper]. A certain policeman
who worked at the police station in *Gangseo-eup* had
digestive problems and was granted a vacation by the chief.
He took his wife, 12-year-old daughter, and 6-year-old son to
Mt. Gangseo Springs and drank its mineral water. During
their vacation, the policeman's wife got up at about two or
three in the morning everyday and went out to the springs in
the silent hours of the night, carrying a small brass kettle
with rice. She lit an "incense of longevity" in front of the "the
spirit of the spring" [Yaksu Daegam was a spirit that the people of
ancient times believed was in the springs] and sacrificed to him with
a sincere heart and prayed, "Let my husband and children
become strong and live long when they drink this mineral
water." The policeman also went out to the spring like his
wife and prayed earnestly. It was summertime then, so they
had put up a mosquito net in the room where the children
were lying down asleep, left the front and back doors open,
left a candlestick with a lit candle in the loft, and went out to

the springs. The wind came in from the front door and went through the back. The mosquito net was pushed by the wind and made contact with the candlestick in the loft [the upper room inside a house]. The mosquito net caught the flame, and the entire house burned down as a result. At that time, the couple was earnestly praying at the mineral waters when they were suddenly startled by the sound of the fire bell. They turned around and discovered that the house they were living in had caught fire. They ran back, but their son and daughter could not escape from the fire and wound up burned to death. As I read the article which said the couple collapsed there and wailed loudly at this great tragedy, I thought to myself, "If those parents had not prayed for blessing from the so-called spirit of the mineral waters, then their beloved children would not have died." They did not seek life where they should have sought it, but instead searched in vain. Because they did not know where the source of life was, they suffered such a calamity.

The Way to Gain Life

In the Scripture the Lord said, "Eternal life is this, knowing the true God who is the only God, and knowing Jesus Christ whom he sent." Therefore, knowing God and knowing Jesus Christ is the way to gain life. We must now recollect and think whether each one of us clearly knows God and Jesus Christ.

When I was conducting catechism for baptism at a certain church, there was a time when I received and asked questions from a 14-year-old girl. At that time I asked that girl, "Who is Jesus?" She replied, "The Son of God." "And who is Jesus' Father?" "It is God." "And who is God's father?" That young girl thought for a long time and answered, "God's father is Jesus," and all the elders erupted in laughter. Of course, this young girl did not know God very well.

We must know Jesus because knowing him is the way to gain life. Once, a catechism for baptism was conducted at a church where an elderly senior also participated. The elderly woman's daughter-in-law taught her the catechism and said to her, "Mother, if you answer exactly as I have taught you when you go to the sanctuary and do the catechism for baptism, you will do just fine." She then said, "If the reverend asks, 'Why did Jesus die?' say that he died for my sins." After that, when the elderly woman was doing her catechism before the church assembly, the reverend asked, "Why did Jesus die?" and the elderly woman replied, "He died for my daughter-in-law's sins." Also, I once asked a certain man, "Why did Jesus die?" He replied, "He got so frustrated that he died for people like me," and the whole congregation laughed loudly. Likewise, there are many people who are not certain if they know God and not sure if they know Jesus.

Only if we know God and know Jesus could we receive this precious life. In what kind of place does the one with this most precious life live? If you look at Revelation 21, it is the City of Zion, the New Jerusalem, magnificently built with gold, silver, and jewels. Brothers, I hope you receive this precious life and enjoy eternal life.

The Spiritual Revelation of the Holy Mountain
Matthew 17:1–8

Preface

According to the records of the Synoptic Gospels, at Caesarea Philippi in the summer of 29 A.D., nine months before Jesus was crucified, he asked his disciples who they thought he was. Peter answered, "Lord, you are the Christ, the Son of the Living God," and Jesus sanctioned the church upon this faith. Some time after this incident, he took Peter, John, and James to the top of Mount Hermon, became transfigured, and conversed with Moses and Elijah. Interpreters of the Bible have many times discussed the transfiguration, but in truth, it is a mysterious fact that we as people cannot fathom. However, if we speak in the realm of what we do know, the transfiguration showed how Jesus would suffer on the cross and would spiritually reveal to the disciples the second coming of the kingdom of glory. And one can conjecture that Elijah and Moses discussed this with Jesus. We, as the next generation, cannot know the specific details, but it is certain that there are numerous things to learn from this spiritual revelation on the holy mountain. Relying on this fact, I would like to explain what I have thought about Christ, the two prophets, and the three disciples.

Things to Learn from the Transfigured Christ

First, we learn about Christ who would suffer. Jesus' transfiguration on the holy mountain is the event that prepared him and the disciples for the suffering of the cross that was clearly approaching before him. Jesus was often hungry, lived without a shelter, suffered, and in the end drank bitter wine on Golgotha for our sake. Even we, the believers, will rightly experience persecution and struggle as we follow in Jesus' footsteps. This is why Peter also said, "Christ suffered for you, leaving you an example, that you should follow in his steps" (1 Peter 2:21). However, among today's Christians, there are many people who are not like that. Thus they attend church if it suits their fame, conduct, or business, but when they encounter a small trouble, many become disappointed, discouraged, and leave. It is absolutely pivotal that we leave this cowardly place, face the cross, and proceed to follow Jesus.

Second, we will wait for Jesus who will come again to reign

in the kingdom of glory. Jesus displaying his glory on the holy mountain signifies the second coming of glory, and he revealed this to the disciples in a vivid reality. Based on my spiritual experience and careful examination of the Bible, I believe that the Lord's second coming is imminent.

Among Jesus' warning of the second coming is the parable of the ten virgins. The five wise virgins were prepared, knowing that the bridegroom would come quickly. On the other hand, the five foolish virgins did not prepare, thinking that the bridegroom would be late. Thus, they could not enter the banquet. Even if you look simply at this parable, we see that his believers must always be prepared since Jesus will not come late.

Therefore, it is not that the believers' faith in the second coming is very faint. As a matter of fact, these days there are many believers who consider the second coming to be beyond their wildest dreams. Is today's church the wise virgin or the foolish virgin? To preoccupy itself in social improvement, the church gets involved in movements and businesses; as a result, it becomes secularized day by day. It does not evangelize, nor does it even pray. Rather, evangelism or prayer is being disdained by the believers of Shinto. Is this the state of the church that has faith in Jesus' second coming? Pastor—elder—deacon—everyone! Where is today's church going? It is not only the Joseon church but the churches of the world that are dozing off like the foolish virgin. Whether the church snoozes or doesn't, the Jesus who will come again will come again.

Even when we take a look at the omens appearing in the world, there are many incidents that one should not see as common. When Jesus was in the world, two people— Caiaphas and Annas—were the high priests of Judah. This was illegal, as it broke the one-person system. At the same time, it indicated the end times of Judah. Likewise, if two people also become Christ, it is the omen of the end times— one would be the true Christ and the other the Anti-Christ. No one will be able to point out who the Anti-Christ is, but there is no secret in the Anti-Christ's advent. Who will go against it and say it does not apply to the prophecy in Isaiah 60 that "Judah's great masses will return"? That is why believers must look and carefully examine it biblically, or watch the omens of the times and hope in the Lord's second coming while being alert and praying.

The Thing to Learn About the Two Prophets Who Appeared on the Holy Mountain

It is said that Moses and Elijah are the two witnesses in Revelation chapter 11 who would appear for three and a half

years. Since Moses was the intercessor for all of Judea, he
represented the Jews, and since Elijah was the prophet of the
northern country of Israel, which was half Jewish and half
Gentile, he represented the Gentiles; thus it is thought that
these two witnesses met on the holy mountain to represent
the Jews and the Gentiles. One could also think that Moses
came to be resurrected since he was already deceased, and
Elijah came to this holy mountain to be transfigured since he
had gone up to heaven in the flesh.

1. There are two things we can learn from Moses. The first
is that as the law appeared through Moses, Moses is, in other
words, the embodiment of the commandments. As Moses
had become the commandments for the Jews, we also
represent the commandments for the unbelievers. When
Paul says, "You are the letters of Christ" (2 Corinthians 3:2),
it means we are to be the holy commandment, capable of
being models for the unbelievers so that we testify to Christ.
Are the believers of the present day truly representing the
commandment to the unbelievers? Twenty years ago in
Pyeongyang, people of debauchery, and even those who
drank alcohol, feared the believers of Jesus and were
ashamed to stand before them. One time, there was an
incident when a woman who had been attending the Winter

Sacrifice [Winter Sacrifice (*dongjei*); people of a village offering a sacrifice to the spirit that guards the village] saw a believer and ran away. A strong intent to train *gisaeng* [girls that were trained to entertain men by singing and dancing]was instead directed to the establishment of a school for girl, and a shaman was transformed into a *gweonchal* [someone entrusted with the duties of watching over the believers' family and visiting them at home] in the church. A few of them are still living. Nevertheless, how is it now? When I tried to evangelize a blind fortune-teller, he told me, "Since many from the church come to me to have their fortunes told, I don't need to give up exorcism or divination and enter the church." Doesn't that mean there is someone among the believers who has gone back to serving idols? Now, aren't drunkards recommending alcohol to elders, elders offering cigarettes to guests, and rounds of *mah-jak* [a traditional Chinese gambling game] becoming common? Pastor, elder, deacon, student, members of the church—how can we be the letters of Christ this way, and how can we represent the holy commandments to the unbelievers?

Second, what we should learn from Moses is that Moses died and was buried, according to the historical account of Deuteronomy 34. When Jesus suffered on the cross, I believe that Moses was resurrected as one person among many holy people who rose again from the grave (Matthew 28:13). Just as Moses died once and lived again, we, too, must die physically and be spiritually transformed once again, and become gentle and humble people. Even in the meetings with company such as a general assembly or sessions, one should not exercise hot-bloodedness without caution. The hot blood of a believer must die and the inner person must be transformed anew.

2. Elijah is the one who was transformed into an immortal body and ascended to heaven on a chariot of fire. The reason Elijah is called the prophet of fire is that he threw an officer, who had fifty soldiers under his order, into the fire, burned sacrifices by lowering the fire of God onto Mount Carmel, and caught and killed 450 prophets of Baal. Observing his intense, fiery character, God answered him with fire, and later he ascended to heaven riding on a chariot of fire. Thus, the title "the prophet of fire" is appropriate.

From Elijah, we wish to model an intensely fiery holy heart, a sacrifice that receives the answer of spiritual fire, and the incident of riding a chariot of fire. We must also have passionate faith and prayer worthy of receiving answers, and we must remain in the Holy Spirit that is like the chariot of fire. All you who have been entrusted with sacred professions! Brothers and sisters! Do you have this kind of diligence? Or prayer? Are you truly riding on the chariot of fire now? They say that there are fifteen thousand believers now (Syowa 5th year, 1930) [Syowa, more commonly, "Showa", is the Japanese name of the era of Emperor Hirohito of Japan, 1926–1989] in Pyeongyang, including the ten thousand Presbyterian believers and almost five thousand in another denomination, but it seems that their enthusiasm has cooled down. Their heat of the spirit has cooled down. A believer that cannot become Christ's letter falls. A church with subsided passion is destined to be ruined. Pyeongyang Church, where are you heading? What are you saying we should do with this in the future?

The Three Disciples' Three Insufficiencies

Peter receives an amazing spiritual revelation at the top of the holy mountain. He tries to build three tents on the holy mountain so that he could live there for a long time with Jesus, Moses and Elijah. However, the three insufficiencies of the three disciples are revealed. We have learned of the goodness of Jesus and the two prophets, but there are also aspects from the three disciples' mistakes we may also learn to be cautious about.

First, their insufficiency was that they wanted to live there forever because they confused the spiritually transformed

world of the holy mountain as an eternal kingdom of heaven.
The mountain only presented an image of the kingdom of
the millennium and not its real sphere. Even in the present
day believers wish to establish a civilized world by improving
society instead of believing in the spiritually glorious heaven
which will be established at Jesus' second coming. The
church therefore throws itself into the cultural movement in
the name of "utopia" [literally, "heaven on earth"], and this is a
colossal mistake. The world seemed to be peaceful during
Noah's time, but in the midst of people's marriages,
establishment of houses, and cultivation of land, weren't
they judged by God when the flood came? Westerners,
having succeeded at a material civilization in modern times,
established an ideal world full of physical pleasures and
boasted that this is heaven on earth. But at the sound of one
young man's gunshot in Serbia [a reference to June 28, 1914, when
a Serbian youth assassinated the Austrian Crown Prince and his wife in
Sarajevo; this resulted in Austria and Serbia's declarations of war and
ignited the First World War], wasn't the dream of pleasure
shattered, and the bloody tragedy of twenty million people
unfolded? Where is the man-made mountain [Tower of
Babel] of Babylon now? Where is the royal palace of *Jin Si
Hwang* [the royal palace built by Qin Shi Huang—Qin Dynasty—in 212
A.D. in the western region of Sian, Sansi Province] and the Temple

of Artemis [Ademi Jeongak is the Temple of Artemis in Ephesus] in Ephesus now? And where are the civilizations of Egypt and Silla? Human constructions and secular culture are left in ruins. Therefore, a person's health and a family's happiness are out of our reach. For us, there is no permanent establishment on the earth other than Jesus' second coming.

Second, their mistake was that they considered Jesus to be at the same level as Moses and Elijah, and they tried to wait equally upon the two prophets and Jesus in the three tents. At least the three disciples treated Jesus equally to the prophets—but one can see that the believers of this world do not even consider Jesus as respectfully as they would Edison the inventor, let alone someone with a lot of wealth.

Whatever the case may be with the person's faith, they can have a tombstone carved and erected for them if they pay the money. Whatever the case with the person's character, they can be seated on a high platform and worshipped if they only have money. Isn't the present-day church falling into an age of worshipping the golden calf? And they do not even treat the Bible as respectfully as science. Everyone! If a scholarly doctor and a divine pastor were sitting here in one place, who would you bow your head to? Today, when you listen to the list of qualifications a church looks for in a minister, these so-called "qualifications" do not signify a spiritual capability but appearance, scholarship, educational history and skill. Alas! There will surely be wrath upon the era when Jesus is treated harshly by the believers, the Bible is disparaged by the church, and a truthful person is cast aside. Brothers and sisters, you must properly lift up Jesus as God and believe the Bible as the word of God.

Third, their mistake was that they only thought of their own spiritual pleasure and did not look back at the people below the mountain. Below the mountain, humankind is rotting inside a cloud of dust [Literally, *hongjinmanjang* has these connotations: a loud, chaotic world where there is only suffering and noise and no truth or happiness]. They are still unable to understand Jesus and the fellow brethren who only have vulgar fights say, "I am high and you are low." Also, can't you hear the children suffering and moaning under evil spirits? Disregarding this and wanting to continue their life on the holy mountain by themselves is so-called "spiritual self-righteousness." This kind of person must go to Paul and learn the ethics of faith of "Take each others' burdens" (Philippians 1:4), and "be concerned for your fellow brethren" (Romans 9:2).

Among fellow believers these days, some that have begun living adequately and established a higher status after receiving Christianity have forgotten all the sufferings from before. They have forgotten the lessons of Jesus, become proud, disdainful, and unsympathetic towards others. They must reconsider their actions. When our faith is strengthened, we must help those whose faith is weak, and when my living or my status improves, I must help those who are more in need than I am, and we must become believers who carry out the Lord's will.

The spiritual world of the holy mountain granted the highest form of evidence for the disciples' faith. The contemporary believers must have this kind of evidence in faith as well. On a faith that follows Jesus' footsteps to Golgotha and waits with a ready heart for Jesus who will come again in a kingdom of glory, this kind of real evidence of the spiritual world will also appear. Just as Moses became the commandment to the Jews, we must also become the commandment to humankind that does not believe and become Christ's letter. In such a life of faith, these real evidences of the spiritual world will appear. Also, for the believers who use the three disciple's insufficiencies as a mirror and lift up Jesus as God, they will be granted an amazing experience. Truly, these words from the clouds will be quietly heard in our spirits: "This is my beloved son, whom I have chosen. Listen to him." We must be upright on this faith of amazing experience and become believers who listen to the words of Jesus and obey.

A Salvation in a Moment
—Five Factors Necessary for Salvation—
Luke 23:39–43

A few years ago in Great Britain, a large ocean liner called the Titanic was built. While on its maiden voyage, it hit a giant iceberg and buried 3,000 passengers in the waves [In 1911, the British White Star Line made its first passenger ship. While making its maiden voyage from England's South Hampton harbor to America's New York harbor, the ship crashed into an iceberg in the waters of Newfoundland and was sunk in 2 hours and 40 minutes. Out of 2208 passengers, 1513 people were killed. Rev. Gil's number is incorrect]. As I think of it, if the captain of the ship saw the iceberg coming toward them with a telescope just a few minutes earlier, he could have been preparing the ship so that it would not make contact with the iceberg. But the captain's momentary negligence sacrificed the lives of 3,000 people.

A while ago, a certain newspaper posed a question with a prize on the line: "How should we save people who go to the bridge of the Han River to commit suicide?" One of the answers chosen for the prize was the following: "One could call the person on his way to die, and tell him that he must urgently speak with him and that he should wait just a moment." Those urgent words of "wait a moment" would make that person stop in his footsteps and one could save him if he quickly went and persuaded him out of it. With a moment's negligence one loses a multitude, and with a moment's persuasion one could save another. Therefore, the matter of one's life and death does not demand a long time but only a moment.

When you read this biblical passage, this robber receiving salvation was also an event that happened in just a moment on the cross. Thus, the salvation of the soul also occurs in one moment. However, while this thief received his salvation in a moment, it has been a difficult thing to achieve for all of time. Therefore, one must have the five necessary factors of contrition, faith, evidence, hope, and earnest request in order to receive salvation.

Contrition

Generally, when a person's flesh is close to death, the heart easily becomes extremely cruel because it has absolutely no hope. Even when one has done good things, who can hold on to him now, and what good would that be for him? This is why the robber on the left cruelly slandered and persecuted the Lord. But the robber on the right said, "We are receiving this punishment that is appropriate for us." Such are words from his heart, which had deeply repented. Adam's sin did not last longer than thirty minutes but this evil has been handed down generations for thousands of years. If he had a repentant heart in that moment of sin, people of the world would not have become this corrupted. Therefore, there is only one way to salvation—through contrition.

Trusting and Relying

It was not only that he was contrite; he also had a deep faith in the Lord. He said, "Though you endure this punishment, do you not fear God? This man has done nothing wrong." He surely believed in the Heavenly Father, and this is also proof that he truly believed in the righteousness of the Lord. In view of the situation at that time, there are two reasons why it was difficult to rely on the Lord.

First, it was truly difficult to believe in the Lord based on his predicament. On the whole, I would trust in others only when they are better off than I. What disciple would have believed in and followed Jesus during his ministry if he had been persecuted and condemned by others, without performing any miracles and holy wonders? When this man, as a thief, looked at the Lord, he saw that he was not even a little bit better off than him. Even though the Lord was enduring a punishment that was much more severe, and there was nothing in him that was worth relying on, the thief deeply believed and relied on the Lord in this situation—how admirable is that? Second, based on his own predicament it was completely difficult to believe. It is easy for anyone's faith to fail when they experience hardship. Even though his blood vessels were cut off and he was at the brink of losing consciousness, he still had a firm sense of trust.

Evidence

It is easy to praise a person when he has status and power, but this period in a person's life is the most frightening time. All the elders, priests, tribunes of cohorts, centurions, and many crowds aside from them all nailed the Lord on the cross. The great mood surrounding him was like a moment when the blade of death glimmers before your eyes in a thirst for blood that reaches the sky. In this moment of terror and fear, the robber confidently testified, "This man has done nothing wrong." In this declaration, there was a deep intention of defeating the extreme wickedness and atrocity of those who were nailing the righteous man Jesus. And on this cross, where even the disciples—those that had loved and followed the Lord—had all fled, how could he have given such a respectful and strictly fair testimony? This moment's testimony of one sentence was better than a testimony in a hundred words during ordinary times. This is an extremely important factor in salvation.

Hope

This person had an eternal hope. He earnestly requested of the Lord, "Remember me when you come into your kingdom." This is an eternal and majestic hope. People nowadays generally lose that hope when they endure hardship. However, even in the midst of pain from a punishment on the infinite cross, he came to have a great hope. This hope allowed him to gain salvation.

Requesting Earnestly

Look at just how this person earnestly requested of the Lord. There was nothing in his prayer that was not answered and nothing he did not receive in his earnest request. Thus, requesting earnestly is an important factor in gaining salvation. The prayer of a believer has the power to move the Heavenly Father.

The thief who repented had the five great factors mentioned above. He was immediately granted complete salvation, and therefore Jesus confidently permitted him to be with him in paradise.

Sanctification 2.6 (1936.6)

Love is the Seed of Paradise
1 Peter 4:1–11

There isn't anyone who sees a blossom and then spits on it and scorns it. When one sees a beautifully blossoming flower, one becomes intoxicated by its wonderful fragrance and one's mood becomes refreshed. In the same way, there is not one person in the entire world who would think of a person that loves them as an enemy. After all, everyone likes to be loved. In that way, love is the seed of paradise. How can one be a seed of paradise? "The most necessary thing is to love one another with enthusiasm." And love is greater than anything else. It is the most important thing for an individual, between spouses, between father and son, in society, or among nations—love is greater than anything else in the entire world. Love is the greatest thing even in heaven. Just as air surrounds the place where animals and plants live, the New Jerusalem, where one lives in a glorified body, is surrounded by love. Hell is the place filled with hatred, and heaven is the place abundant in love.

1 Corinthians 13 exalts the value of love: "If I speak the

language of angels, prophesy, and master all knowledge, and if I have faith to move a mountain, and I give everything to help the poor, and even if I let me body be burnt, if I have not love it is useless; therefore it is written—faith, hope, and love—these three will always be, but the greatest of these is love." Prophesying will be done away with, tongues will cease, and even knowledge will be invalidated. But only love will never fail. We long for heaven. It is because heaven is a place full of love. If we engage our family, society, and nation with love, then the world would immediately become a heaven on earth. In that way, love is the seed of the garden of paradise. Then, what kind of love could become the seed of paradise? It is a "love of zeal." There are many kinds of love in the Bible: there is great love and small love, hot love and lukewarm love, temporary love and eternal love.

Decades ago at the time of the Great War, three thousand soldiers were put on a warship. While they were leaving to conquer Germany, they were shipwrecked by a German destroyer ship. Among them, a serviceman of faith sprung out from the water and obtained a piece of plank wood and, regarding it as his life, clung on the piece of wood and swam. Some time later, one seaman appeared along the way saying, "Let me ride also," and the two of them went, taking turns. But along the way to London harbor, both of them became completely exhausted to the point of fainting. The seaman that believed in God said, "If we try to save both of us, we'll both end up dying—you take it and go alone." The unbeliever urged, "You have the right to decide first, so you take it." But the believer didn't listen, saying, "If I die now I will have received salvation but if you die now you'll receive destruction, so at all costs please ride this and live, believe in Jesus, receive salvation and let us meet in heaven. If you see my parents in a certain sanctuary in England, urge them, 'love one another ardently'." Having said that, he sank deep into the water and died. That friend wept loudly and repented, and he eagerly experienced the truth of the redemption of the cross. That seaman safely arrived at the port and, seeking the sanctuary, told the pastor what had happened. The pastor told that brother to speak at the pulpit. Shedding tears, he explained the situation for a long time, and when he delivered the words "love ardently," a thousand believers wept and confessed on their own that they had not loved, and a great revival arose. Therefore, the members of that church began to love each other, and they built a paradise. Rightfully, let's love each other with ardor so that our families and our churches may become the flowering gardens of paradise.

Who is the one to build a paradise? It is the one who loves

the other. It is not the one who excels in knowledge, or the one of noble status, but the one who loves the other in the Lord Jesus. Everyone! Haven't you heard of the saying, *dokjangnanmyeong* [Literally, No sound comes out of a one-hand clap] Surely, one cannot grind even one kernel of grain with only one milling stone. One must absolutely have two sides. Of course, God loves us. But if humans don't love each other, we cannot dare to receive God's love, nor can we realize it. Therefore more than anything, we must become a people who love. The ones who love! These are the people of heaven. One who does not love is a child of hell, a child of the devil. One who loves can break the power of hell and build a paradise—so let us all become people who love.

What is the benefit of love? Love hides innumerable sins. When one has love, another's weaknesses disappear before their eyes. For example, an innocent baby strikes a mother's cheek but the mother laughs. That is because she has love. There is truth to the saying that a porcupine always thinks its baby's hair is soft.

When I once took a stroll in the fields, I saw that fish scales on top of a plate had created a world of rainbows. I looked carefully at the plate but only saw a small fish. I realized that the sun's seven colors were shining through the fish. I prayed, "Lord! Let my eyes become eyes of love, absorbing

the light of Jesus' sun, that I may see my brothers."
Depending on where you rest your eyes when standing in the
Manmulsang [the all creatures statue] area of the Guemgang
Mountains [often called the Diamond Mountains in English], you can
see something that looks like a general, a young child, or a
lion. Because the formations take the shapes of all kinds of
creatures, they are called "all creatures statue [*manmulsang*],"
and a person's eyes are exactly *Manmulsang*. Whatever we
do, let's see everything with eyes of love.

Look at my eyes. Are they somewhat big? Those who know
me see them as ordinary, but those who do not know me see
them as strange. Our church believers see my eyes and say
they are like the eyes of an angel and that they are like
fireworks (actually, they sparkle because of the high
prescription of my glasses). That's why, they tell me, they
cannot help but admit their sins. But people who don't know
me call me large-eyed or frog-eyed [literally, "a person with eyes
like large water drops."] Then, have my eyes changed? No. It is
because the eyes of the person who sees me are different. It
is because the former sees with eyes of love and the latter
sees with eyes of criticism.

Let's say that your daughter-in-law becomes pitted with
smallpox. When you look at her with eyes of love, you say the
sunken, pitted marks are filled with blessings. But if you look

at her with eyes of hatred, you see the scarred face and call it a pock-face and crater-face. Then does that mean the face has changed into that of a turkey? No. The eyes of the beholder see a turkey. Just like this, "Love hides all sins" (1 Peter 4:8).

Today's church has no love; therefore believers fight with each other. Claiming the constitution or a principle, they only seek out a person's faults. If they love each other there wouldn't be this kind of schism. Society is that way, too. There is only fighting between brothers, and because they simply have to produce bloody tragedies through power struggles, there is no peace. Ah—if only there was the love like that of Jesus, the love of Paul, the love of Stephen in this church and this society, then in our peninsula, the beautiful flower of love would come into a full bloom and we would achieve an earthly paradise. "The more dust is kicked up, the more it smells; the more a perfume is sprayed, the more it gives off a strong smell." Let's not reveal another's faults and give off a foul odor, but let us lift up one's merits and spread only the fragrance of love. When we do this, this world will automatically become a flowering garden.

To Whom Shall We Go?
John 6:68–69

Peter's answer

After Jesus fed the five thousand with five loaves of bread and two fish in the wilderness of Bethesda, he said to the multitudes following him, "Do not follow me for the sake of food that decays." And he said that one has to eat his flesh and drink his blood to live eternally. The crowds who wanted to make Jesus king and solve their political and economic problems listened to Jesus' words and were disappointed because their expectations were different from his. Thus, all the disciples besides the twelve apostles withdrew. Jesus asked the remaining twelve disciples, "Would you like to leave as well?" and Peter answered, "To whom shall we go?" This answer showed that there was nowhere else to go, and that they would follow only Jesus.

Nowhere to Go
1. Shall we follow money and go to the rich (James 1:11)?
A rich man of olden days, Seoksung [a wealthy man of Seojin, in

China, who became rich through voyage and trade], was murdered by King Jo merely because of a beautiful woman. The later generation judged it as, "He only planned to gain the treasure and didn't know how to take care of his body." Also, there is the phrase, "Riches cannot save a person—after all, only water flows fleetingly at Geumgokweon" [Namely, riches are of no use. Geumgokweon was the name of Seoksung's villa].

2. Shall we follow power and go to an authority (Ecclesiastes 1:2–3, 17)?

(1) Even if one is a hero, he cannot save his own body. Even Hangwu of "spirit and vigor enough to overcome the world and pluck mountains" was defeated by Paegong [the first emperor of the Han Dynasty, Yubang, 247–195 B.C.] and committed suicide on the river bank of a country named Oh. Even Napoleon, who shook an entire generation, breathed his last on a lonely island while in prison—so where would he receive the strength to save others?

(2) Should we go to the scholars (1 Corinthians 1:19)? The learning of the olden days does not compare to modern knowledge, and today's materialism cannot become tomorrow's knowledge. Then, how can learning save a person?

3. Shall we go to a religious man?

Confucius did not know about the afterlife, and he said, "I am ignorant of life, so how can I know death?" Buddha died and Lao-tzu and Chuang-tzu are nothing, so how can one ask about eternal life? *The Book of Odes* says, "The ideology of old generals is bloated in nothingness and holds to empty teachings; Confucius and Mencius thought only they were right and did not know how to learn higher ideologies" [literally, *Nojang'gigeogongyudo* and *gongmaeng'yujonbulhakseon*, meaning, "such are empty teachings that cannot save people."]

Believe in Jesus and Know

"Lord, you have the words of eternal life. To whom shall we go" (John 6:68)? One must know the Lord of eternal life. In verse 69 it says, "We believe and know that you are the Holy One of God," thus, we come to Jesus with "faith" and "knowledge," and receive salvation and live forever in Him.

1. Believing in Jesus
(1) Believing in his name (John 1:12)
(2) Believing in his work (John 3:2)
(3) Believing in his word (John 6:68–69)

2. Knowing Jesus means Knowing Jesus through faith

(1) We must come to know the savior who saves us from sin and death. "There is no other name under heaven given to men by which we must be saved" (Acts 4:12).

(2) We must come to know him as the Lord of grace and truth (John 1:14).

(3) We must come to know him as the Lord of life. "Eternal life is this: that they may know you, the one and only God, and Jesus Christ, whom you have sent" (John 17:3; 6:68–69).

Come to Jesus

Brothers, sisters! If the Lord asks, "Do you want to leave too?" how will you answer? "Lord, to whom shall we go? You have the words of life." Come to the Lord of life and receive eternal life. "Whoever comes to me I will never drive away" (John 6:37). "Seek the Lord while he may be found; call on him while he is near. Let the wicked forsake his way and the evil man his thoughts. Let him turn to the Lord" (Isaiah 55:6–7).

A Life in Faith 9.3 (1940.3)

III. The Life of Christians

Concerning the Test of the Fruit of the Knowledge of Good and Evil
Genesis 2:16–17; 3:1–24

Theologically, the fact that God has created the fruit of the knowledge of good and evil is a problematic issue. This is because one may ask, "For what reason did the omniscient, almighty God create the fruit of the knowledge of good and evil when man would fail to obey him and sin?" However, God did not mean for humankind to fail. There are five kinds of tests: 1) Satan's test, 2) man's test, 3) a test of objects, 4) tests received on one's own, and 5) God's test. The test of the fruit of the knowledge of good and evil is, just as we read in our Scripture, Satan's test. Satan's test is a test of evil will, but God's test is a test given to humankind so that it would lead a pleasant life. In the Epistle of James, it says that God does not test with evil nor is he tempted by evil. Just as people do not wish to ruin their children, as a merciful god he absolutely does not desire to destroy humankind. God had four purposes in testing man with the fruit of the knowledge of good and evil.

It was to Display His Authority and Sovereignty Over Heaven and Earth.

If there is a god, he would be sovereign on heaven and earth. If he were not the sovereign of the universe, he would be a powerless god. Therefore, without the fruit of the knowledge of good and evil, he could not be the sovereign of heaven and earth. Figuratively speaking, if someone first discovered the earth that was not governed by a master, he would become its master by right of priority according to international law. But if he were to come to a certain corner and unexpectedly discover a signboard which recorded, "Everything can be used at your discretion, but a certain one thing is not permitted," this person would realize, rather, that there is a master here who came first, and he would surely know that he was the second master, or that he was only a steward of that first master. In the same way, God made the fruit of the knowledge of good and evil to make known that he was the sovereign of heaven and earth.

It was to Make the World a Garden of Peace

However, it is easy for someone to retort, "But rather, didn't unhappiness and suffering enter the world as the result?" I respond to that question in this way. Figuratively speaking, it is like the necessity of autocracy for an uncivilized people and the limiting of freedom for a young child. In China, a number of prominent figures each claim to be great and create their own worlds; and when they fight each other, the blood of an innocent population is spilled. This fruit of the knowledge of good and evil is God's majestic law of justice for human peace. When humans submit to this, they are able to have peace. Our first ancestors failed the test of the fruit of the knowledge of good and evil, but from it we have learned the lesson of obedience. Now, the world has order and so do family, society, and the country.

It was to Entrust an Important Duty to Humankind

In order to entrust an important duty to a person, a test is necessary. In the presidential election in the United States, people vote after testing the candidates. They listen to speeches, they survey their behavior, and they test them in many other different ways. After all, if they want to raise up the world's second master, he must be tested. It is easy to retort, "How can one not fail a difficult test?" I answer this in this way: "The test of the fruit of the knowledge of good and evil is an extremely easy test. God does not test humans above what they can handle. When one takes a test to enter school, one takes it with the educational knowledge they have received from the school they have graduated from. They are not tested based on something they have not learned. So then, if there is a student who fails the test, whose fault is it? Naturally, the student has no choice but to take responsibility for it. If there is a sign on the side of the road in a dangerous zone that reads, "This place is dangerous; do not enter," and despite it one proceeds to go and on their way falls and dies, with whom does that error lie? Naturally, it is with the pedestrian himself. Therefore, being told they are able to eat everything except the fruit of one tree is not a difficult to do.

It was to Give Freedom to Humankind.

If God desires to make a human that does not commit sin, he would be able to. But a human that is obedient because they are made to submit would be mechanical and worthless. A clock matches to a certain time because it is made to match that way, and a rooster crows at dawn because God made it that way. Behold! There is no advancement for mechanical creations, and no development. A nest that a magpie would make in the old days is exactly the same as a nest that a magpie would make today. But because humankind has freedom, there is advancement and progress. Mechanical subordination is not obedience. If God wanted to make humans so that they could not eat the fruit of the knowledge of good and evil, he could have. But then man would not have been free and become complete as the completeness of God that is able to advance ever more.

The claim that the test of the fruit of the knowledge of good and evil is difficult is impossible to accept. If Adam told God that he had failed because the test was too hard, the witnesses to answer him have been innumerable. There was Abraham, Job, and countless prophets aside from them. And what's more, wasn't there our Lord Jesus? Compared to these, the test of the fruit of the knowledge of good and evil was very small. If we throw away our useless doubts about the fruit of the knowledge of good and evil and believe only in Jesus Christ who triumphed over all temptations, we will receive our salvation. Adam failed, but because he was tested to begin with, today we can advance more through submission to God and become complete.

Confess Your Sin and Pray

Sin Blocks Prayer

In Luke 18:13–14, the Lord compares the prayers of the believing tax collector and that of the Pharisees to teach about the attitude of prayer. He teaches that the contrite prayer of the tax collector has been acknowledged as righteous and the prayer of the boastful Pharisee believer has not been granted. And in James 5:16, it is written that if "you tell each other of your sins and pray the Lord will answer you." And in Daniel 9, Daniel lamented and prayed for his sin and the sin of his Israelite people saying, "Lord, forgive my sin and the sin of this people," and the Lord answered at the same time revealing all the provision and hope concerning the future of the Israelite people. Starting a few weeks ago at our Wednesday service, I have continuously preached on the problem of "Lord, are you hearing my prayer?" Until last Wednesday, we have learned that we should pray in unison, pray in faith, and pray after forgiving others' sins. Tonight, we will be thinking about the issue of praying while telling and confessing our sins to each other.

There comes a time when we pray to God but cannot receive answers. This is related to the fact that we have not repented of our sins and confessed them. The Lord said, "Would I become deaf and not hear your prayer? It is not because my hand is short that I cannot save you. Sin blocks you and me that I do not hear you; I shall not save you." God does not answer the prayers of a sinner. Therefore, there are occasionally times when our prayers are blocked. If we were to list our sins now, they would be countless in number and range. But when you point out the sins of today's believers to them, they close their ears. Even John the Baptist, when he first evangelized cried out, "Repent, for heaven is near" and even the Lord said at the very beginning of evangelism, "Repent, for heaven is near" (Matthew 4:17). He said heaven is near but have we already received heaven? Is there really no sin to repent? The fact that we are not secure in our mind, body, and soul, and that the world is in chaos and devoid of righteousness is evidence that there are many people who have yet to confess.

The Sins of the Believers

What is sin? Is only adultery or thieving sin? Can you say that you did not commit sin because you don't have this or that sort of sin? Just as I have written in the catechism,

"Sin is falling short of obeying God's law and violating it."
Everything that is illegal in the Bible is of course a sin.
Knowing how to behave in righteousness and not doing so
is a sin, and not being obedient, and all conduct aside
from faith are all sinful. Why are we still defeated by sin
and unable to receive the fullness of the Holy Spirit when
we believe in Jesus and toil? This is because we are still
sinful. There is sin against God and sin against people;
there is sin that is hidden and sin that is visible; sins we
commit in our hearts and sins we commit verbally;
behavioral sin and familial sin; personal sin, sin concerning
the church, sin concerning society, and many other types
of sin.

Why were the ancient righteous men and prophets
persecuted? They were harmed because they correctly
rebuked the wickedness of the period. Why did the Lord
Jesus suffer on the cross? If the Lord had said only the words
that were pleasant for them to hear he would not have been
harmed by them. Even to this day, if there is one who
correctly warns of the sin of the church, clergy, and believers,
he also would not escape the harm that the prophets
received.

In the Modern Church

Brothers, are you trying to receive grace? Repent and confess. Repent and pray. If innumerable complaints arise as the result of jealous sin, all filthiness appears in sins of lust, deception, slander, oppression—if you commit the sin of being intolerant of your brother and others—if you commit the sins of stinginess, laziness, grieving the Holy Spirit, blocking the Holy Spirit, loving evil, oppressing the righteous—and if you ostracize a righteous man with personal feelings—you will not be granted answers to your prayers even if you pray.

Has our church received grace? If it has, then it would be good; but what happens if it has not received it? Do not say, "It is going well." Doesn't everyone speak of the poor progress of our church? Doesn't it say in Revelation 2, "If you do not repent the light will be moved from that place"? Do you think the Lord would leave the light in our place if our church does not repent? To whom will the sin that corrupts the church go? The Lord will first examine our leaders. How can we not be afraid? Daniel was a more righteous man than us and was a saint, but didn't even he lament his sins and confess? You sinners who hold onto the keys of heaven and do not enter nor allow others to enter, confess, lament, and repent of your sins. Pretending to be a believer for ten, twenty years is not noble; becoming one who confesses and laments is, however, noble.

Does God listen to our prayers? In the time of Jesus, when someone asked a strange question about Pilate mixing the blood of a Galilean in the offering, how did the Lord reply? Jesus said, "Do you think according to your idea that through this Galilean being killed he has more sin than many Galileans? I tell you, it is not so. Only if you do not repent you will all be ruined like this." And in Matthew 11:20–24, he says, "Woe to you, Chorazin! Woe to you, Bethsaida! If the miracles that were performed in you had been performed in Tyre and Sidon, they would have repented long ago in sackcloth and ashes. But I tell you, it will be more bearable for Tyre and Sidon on the Day of Judgment than for you. And you, Capernaum, will you be lifted up to the skies? No, you will go down to the depths. If the miracles that were performed in you had been performed in Sodom, it would have remained to this day. But I tell you that it will be more bearable for Sodom on the Day of Judgment than for you." And he rebukes the city that would not repent. Are we better off than this? Don't we commit the sins of refusing to repent and blaming other brothers, and not forgiving the sins of other brothers? How much better is today's church than the Pharisees?

Confess Hidden Sins and Pray

Before, there were five brothers in a large house in Europe. One day, the oldest son suddenly got a stomachache, suffered and died. Soon after that, all four brothers—second, third, and fourth in succession—suffered and died in the same manner. A doctor was called in to investigate the cause of the illness, and in the end he discovered a poisonous virus spreading in the house. When he decontaminated each room with the disinfectant, the owner opened almost every room for the doctor, but at the very end he did not open one small back room in the corner of the house. When the doctor asked the owner why he wouldn't open this room, the owner said, "People do not easily go in and out of this room so it doesn't matter if we do not fumigate it." The doctor urged him several times to disinfect the room, but the owner did not obey him from start to finish. The doctor felt it regrettable and could not have peace of mind. After that, the owner, his wife, and their youngest son went to a different region to nurture their minds for many months. However, as expected, when they returned, a few days later their youngest son became ill with the same disease as his brothers and left the world. A short time later the owner and his wife also died from the same disease. When the back room in the corner was opened after the entire family was destroyed, lying there were expensive gold and silver treasures completely filling the room. The entire family was wiped out as a result of the family's unwillingness to open and disinfect the small back room full of many precious and valuable things.

We may also have times when we repent and confess small sins only superficially and do not confess deeply hidden sins. Regardless, anyone who hides those sins deep inside a back room and does not repent of them will be ruined by them. Expose all the deeply hidden sins inside of you and confess.

Lastly, there is a need for us to go under the knife to treat our sins. It is easy to fix skin-deep problems, but it is difficult to fix deeply embedded ones. Though my father, brother, mother, and sister knew of the suffering I endured from heart failure about ten years ago, at the time all the general practitioners did not recognize these symptoms. Doctor Keoreulneo in Kyeongseong [an old name for Seoul during the time of Japanese colonization] examined it and said, "There is pus in your intestines so we have no choice but to perform surgery quickly." In a flash, I was admitted to a Christian hospital where four doctors performed surgery to take out a great amount of pus from my insides. Before that surgery other people did not know of my extreme suffering. Before the surgery, others did not know of my excruciating pain. From someone else's view, it did not seem like that serious a disease, but I was enduring such extreme pain that I could not bear it. If I had not received surgery at that time I would have been at the edge of my life. Let's receive the Spirit's surgery on our sin. Confess with lamentation and pray so that you may receive the Holy Spirit's surgery.

The method of receiving forgiveness consists only of two things. That is first confessing the sin you had before entering the faith and repenting and receiving forgiveness from the Lord through faith. Then, second, for the sin you committed after you had faith, you receive forgiveness through lamenting in prayer whenever you think of those sins. 1 John 1:9 says, "If we confess our sins, he is faithful and just and will forgive us our sins and purify us from all unrighteousness." Do not pray only according to regulation. Let us pray so that the movement of the Holy Spirit prevents our prayers from being blocked, so that we can recognize our sins on our own. Then, let us see our sins, confess them and pray as we see them. In this way, let us endeavor until we receive complete forgiveness from the Lord.

The Fragrance of Christ
2 Corinthians 2:12–13

In the Bible, we see many special words dedicated to faithful believers. In some places it says, "You are a priesthood," and in some places, "temple," "living stone," "branch on the vine," "light of the world," and "salt of the earth." In the words of the Bible that we are reading now, the teacher Paul especially denotes us as the "Fragrance of Christ."

One comes to think of ingredients. I have experience studying Oriental medicine and I can therefore discern the general features of ingredients for fragrances. To be this specific incense of Christ, many medicines must be combined. If you look at the time of Exodus in the Old Testament, they always made this fragrance exude in the tabernacle, and it also had many ingredients. If they would mix a few medicines as fragrance used for medicinal purposes then what are the ingredients of Christ's fragrance? The Bible speaks on those ingredients. It clearly speaks of them from Galatians 5:22. There, it says they are "love, joy, peace, patience, kindness, goodness, faithfulness, gentleness and self-control." Then, there are nine ingredients in the fragrance of Christ. If one wisely mixes these well, it drifts from place to place and emits a beautiful fragrance, and the effect of that fragrance is exceptionally great.

Next, let us think about the effect of this beautiful fragrance. The word 'fragrance' sounds very soft in our ears. Then let us think once about its effect and its nature. This fragrance:

1. Passively works to kill. When one wears good fragrance, all germs die. It also eradicates malaria; it is a germicide. Also, the fragrance of Christ has a killing effect.

 a) It kills sin. It eradicates all sins upon entering the core of a person whether they are a believer or an unbeliever. Also, this fragrance

 b) It kills things such as hot blood, temperament and evil hearts. These are like bad germs and poison to whatever they come in contact with. When a place is filled with this fragrance, not one element of the devil is able to stay in it.

2. Actively affects to save. Medically, it has great potency on diseases like paralysis, cerebral hemorrhages and seizures. What would it be like to become the true fragrance of Christ? The effect would be truly immense, because

a) sinners headed toward death would be saved and would attain life to glorify the Lord;

b) the discouraged would be uplifted and led toward hope and delight, and he who suffers from the pang of conscience would be given peace;

c) the arrogant would be made humble and would begin to take after Christ.

If we become the true fragrance of Christ, we would come to lack nothing in serving the Lord. I know a certain person who is not very eloquent. However, I saw him move many people through his virtuous conduct and lead the dying toward the path of life. Let us make efforts to be the true fragrance of Christ, showing the glory of the Lord wherever we go. You many brothers and sisters gathered here, have you become the true fragrance of Christ?

Next, I would like to think about the application of the fragrance of Christ. A fragrance would move our sense of smell through the wind. Then we who are the fragrance of Christ must go and introduce Christ to whichever place, as guided by the heavenly wind of the Holy Spirit. Look at Acts chapter two. Didn't they go to the ends of the earth after receiving the filling of the Holy Spirit, preaching the gospel of Christ? It says it came upon them like a wind, so we also demand this wind of the Holy Spirit. Let's find out, then, the way to use this fragrance.

1. You must actively use it. If you put fragrance in a dresser and leave it, that fragrance would never see the light of day. It must be placed where the wind blows well for it to be used well. Then with what, and how, must we make it move?

a) First, we must move it with prayer. Prayer is the breath of believers. With this we can send our fragrance all the way before the Lord and to all people. The source of what we call spiritual power is all in this. This prayer is not something that only a church staff needs, but school teachers and everyone else as well. Some people try to believe academically, mystically, or willfully. But we endeavor to believe in prayer. The fragrance of knowledge is not very beautiful, but the fragrance of prayer is beautiful. Today's church tries to have success in the work of Christ without prayer, but they all fail.

b) Next move it with the Bible. When we look at our fellow believers, we see that though they come out for everything else, they do not come for Bible studies. Even though all the knowledge of the world cannot give virtues to humankind, the Bible is the word for all people and the word of life. How can a believer who is negligent of this exude the fragrance of Christ? The fragrance of biblical knowledge is beautiful. If we pray, read the Bible, and look after people, they will be moved.

c) Finally, move it through evangelism. When the fire of the Holy Spirit came down thirty years ago, I saw many people evangelizing with wild enthusiasm. At that time, one evangelized whether they were in the car or on the street. Today is the exact opposite and that is why people want church prosperity. That is why we see that churches that gathered hundreds of people in the past have today fallen into an unutterable state. The source of this is in our failure to evangelize. Have we not also received salvation by being evangelized? Then evangelism is not only giving grace to others but is also grace for me. The plan for the revival of today's church is only in this. Look at Daniel 12:3. It says there that "those who teach many people and lead them back to righteousness will shine like the stars forever and ever."

2. Next, if you want to use this fragrance effectively, you must put it through fire. If you do not throw the incense into the fire, that fragrance would not completely spread. Shall I try throwing the nine perfume ingredients that I spoke of a short while ago into the blazing fire of the Holy Spirit? Ah— an inexpressible fragrance will come forth. If we want to emit Christ's fragrance all the time, we must put it in the midst of

the flame of the Holy Spirit. Fragrance gives out great emotions. We can sense this even from far away. Shall we make here a beautiful artificial flower and put it with a real flower? No matter how long we wait, a butterfly or bee will not come near it. But they come easily near a real flower even when they are not asked.

If we have become Christ's true fragrance, wouldn't those people that are dying all around us come before the Lord? But how ineffective are we? What we need at this time is for the Holy Spirit to come down, just as at the time of Pentecost, and change all of us so that we become the Lord's true fragrance. Let us try to be a great glory before God and people. Let us believe in the Lord and pray for the Holy Spirit's arrival.

The Three Great Blessings of the Person in Christ

"Therefore, there is now no condemnation for those who are in Christ Jesus, because through Christ Jesus the law of the Spirit of life set me free from the law of sin and death, that the righteousness of the law might be fully met in us who live according to the Spirit" (Romans 8:2–4).

No Condemnation

When you read Romans 6 and 7, you can see that the Apostle Paul's fight with sin is fierce and acute. His cries of "The wages of sin is death," or "Alas! I am a troubled person," are the most spiritually intense shouts and the greatest spiritual exclamation. Anyone who has had the experience of fighting wickedness would surely feel as if they are watching the last five minutes of the Battle of Waterloo when reading Paul's writings of a spiritual battle in Romans 6 and 7. Paul, who had fought as fiercely as this, declares confidently when he arrives at Romans 8, "Therefore there is now no condemnation for those who are in Christ Jesus."

This is a proclamation of a great victory for all the ages.

Many scholars, besides great figures such as Kode [presumably, an important Bible commentator of the past], say that the phrase "therefore" is a word continuing from chapters 7 and 8, but it can also be words connecting everything from chapters 1–8, or be seen as succeeding the meaning of chapters 5, 6, and 7. When does he mean when he says "now"? It is the "now" of when Jesus, the Messiah permitted to Abraham, returns; it is the "now" of when Jesus dies on the cross, resurrects and ascends, or the "now" of when Paul repents and believes. Moreover, it is the "now" that fights sin and wins. This is why therefore, now "there is no condemnation for those who are in Christ Jesus," for those who have come to belong to Jesus completely, the control, punishment, and the fear of sin are gone. For the soul that has had to say, "Lo, I am a troubled person," the words of "there is no condemnation for those who are in Christ Jesus" are surely the most joyful to hear.

For example, just as one must first catch the train in order to catch someone inside a train, in order to condemn the one who is in Jesus one must first condemn Jesus. But Jesus is absolutely innocent. Even though he took on our sins, he could still overcome evil and be resurrected. And now, the resurrected Jesus cannot be condemned, and no one can condemn the one who is in him. One cannot seize the one inside a city without destroying it; Jesus is our fortress. He is the strong fortress that can never be destroyed. Jesus is our city of refuge. He is the steadfast city of refuge. As long as this fortress, this city of refuge, does not fall, in this fortress I am safe. Inside this city of refuge I am not a sinner. One step outside of the city of refuge I would have been a sinner to be destroyed, but "now" in Jesus I am a righteous man for all eternity. "Who will bring a charge against the people whom God has chosen? It is God who justifies. Who is he that condemns? Christ Jesus, who died and was raised to life again, is at the right hand of God and is also interceding for us" (Romans 8:33–34). This is the first blessing of the one who is in Christ Jesus.

Escaping from the Pathway of Death

The words, "through Christ Jesus the law of the Spirit of life set me free from the law of sin and death," are an explanation regarding "non-condemnation" in verse 1 as well as words that indicate more so the provision that frees us from the law of death. Thus, this escape from the line of death is the second blessing of the one who is in Christ.

'Law' from the phrase "the law of sin and death" is a rule but also a principle. Humans live out their lives in the law of sin and principle of death. It is a principle and a law that one cannot escape. Just as a train can only go by the way of two railroad tracks, a person cannot escape the two railroad tracks of sin and death. The direction of the railroad tracks of sin and death leads to the dark underworld, and its final destination is hell. Also, foolish men and women cannot escape these two railroad tracks—not even a wise man can escape these two principles. Thus, all people are sinners and those destined to die. "Alas, I am a troubled person. Who will bring me out of this swamp of sin and death?"

God does what humans cannot do readily, and He does what cannot be easily done by the power of the law—that is, what Jesus Christ his son does by the cross. It can be done by what is in Christ Jesus—the life of the Holy Spirit of life and the law. A train charging toward the swamp of sin and death crashed into another different, large train in the opposite direction. This train was coming out of the line of life and of the Holy Spirit. The train derailed and overturned. The people on this train moved onto the new train and began to go into the opposite direction, through the railway of life and of the Holy Spirit. Jesus died at the crash of the law of life and of death, the law of the Holy Spirit and of sin. However, through Jesus' resurrection, the law of life became victorious and it now moves forward by the law of the Holy Spirit. Our

lives also have been overturned in this clash of the new law
with the former law of sin. We are now saved anew and
living according to the law of the Holy Spirit.

Therefore, the one who is in Christ Jesus has escaped the
railroad track of sin and death and has now transferred to
the track of life and the Holy Spirit. Adam came by the law of
sin and death and Jesus came by the law of life and the Holy
Spirit. Thus, the one who is born of Adam charges down the
railroad line of Adam but the one who is in Jesus shall ride in
the line of Jesus. For the direction of this track of the Spirit
and life is heaven and its final stop the world where one
enjoys unending rest.

Righteousness Fulfilled

"For us, who do not act according to that flesh and live by
the Spirit," the righteousness of the law is completed, thus
the fulfillment of righteousness is the third blessing of the
one who is in Jesus.

The one who does not act according to the flesh is the
person who does not go down the path of sin; it is the person
who acts according to the Spirit, namely the one who goes
down the path of the Spirit and life. The completion of
righteousness is given to this kind of person. Here, the
righteousness of the law is not limited to the laws and

customs of the Jews or Moses' law; it is the heavenly law of Jesus who said, "I did not come to abolish the law, but to complete it." It is not that one is made righteous by the law, but that "righteousness" is shown through the law. This is the righteousness that one can receive by the cross of Jesus; it is the righteousness that can only be fulfilled by the Spirit. It is the righteousness that is poured upon the one who thirsts and hungers in yearning for it.

For the Christian, there is not just the passive aspect of non-condemnation or being free from the way of death, but also the active aspect of attaining the fulfillment of righteousness. Speaking figuratively about the train that I just mentioned, it is not only an empty train that is free from the way of death but also the train full of righteousness that is moving along the path of life. Humankind, even while charging down the road of sin, has the fear of justice on its face, and deep down in its heart, feels a demand for righteousness. "Let justice roll on like a river, righteousness like a never-failing stream" (Amos 5:24). The people of the world are leaving God. Without any righteousness, they charge down the road of the flesh. They do not have righteousness but for the one who is in Christ Jesus, righteousness will be given. For us who are going down the railroad track of the Spirit, he will grant us the fullness of righteousness.

The Five Great Essentials of the Believer
1 Corinthians 4

Any product of this world is made with a shape. Without a shape, a product cannot be complete. Just like this, when a believer models himself after Christ he becomes perfect. So then, we will speak of five great essentials that the believer must properly model.

Language

Being a model in speech is an element of the believer. Through words one can proclaim the gospel, and through words one can chase evil spirits. Through words one can exert influence over a person, or, conversely, one can ruin a person, a family, or a nation. Through cunning words, Satan brought destruction upon the relationship between God and man, and in the age of China's Six States, Sojin, with a tongue as long as three *chi* [one *chi* is about 3 cm], made peace in the Six States and became the premier of its empire. This is the difference between killing a person by the sword and murdering with words: committing murder with a weapon is limited and only affects a few people, but one can easily kill the entire world with words. Thus, words are all the more severe than weapons. That is why James called his tongue "the fire that destroys the world with its flame" and Paul called God's word "the weapon of righteousness that is used as liberty," and in the Book of Hebrews it is called a "double-edged sword."

There is, in our world, inequality and conflict, discord within the family, and also much confusion in society and the nation. When one takes a good look at the source, almost all of them have been caused by words. Indeed, one is able to put the entire world into chaos through words. Moreover, all kinds of incidents are rising up in the church. But having been a believer for forty years and a minister for twenty years, and having experienced and observed these incidents, I see that the words are the cause of every single scandal. Ah—words can destroy others and ruin your own life. For that reason, a true gentleman—no, a believer—must be careful with words and be a role model in speech. Peter said, "Whoever loves his own life and wants to see good days must keep his tongue from evil and his lips from deceitful speech" (1 Peter 3:10). Among present believers, there was one that easily and frequently spread such lies. The words he spoke, though they were like truths, were lies.

A parable: One day, a certain farmer was on his way to a market to sell his cow when he met a friend. "Where are you going?" "I'm going to the market to sell my cow." "Oh, is that so? I'm going to the market to buy a cow." After talking to each other about the cow, they exchanged many different questions and answers. Setting the price, they made a transaction. When they were bidding each other farewell, the one who sold the cow said to the one who bought it, "That cow is all good, but there is one flaw of which you should know. If the fact that this cow will not step onto wood can even be called a flaw, then that's its flaw." The one who bought the cow said, "It's not a big flaw if it's just that the cow doesn't step onto wood." He bought it anyways and took it home, and after he returned, he saw that it plowed well, it carried loads well, and it had a fine disposition. He was very pleased. One day he loaded it with salt and was about to cross a great river, but when it was about to get on the ferry this cow would absolutely not get on. It shook off its load of salt and ran away into the mountains. This person went through all sorts of hardships and took great pains to catch the cow. The next day, after he had caught it, he sought the friend who had sold him the cow. "That cow has this great flaw, but what reason is there between friends that you did not let me know?" and he rebuked him. But as he did so that friend replied, "Ah, didn't I tell you carefully at that time? That the cow is all good, but he has one flaw, and that it would not step onto wood? Isn't the ferry made of wood?" Like so, though it seems like truth, there are times when it becomes lies. Among church members, there are those who say lies like these in order to entrap the minister. They say, "That pastor travels on the road a lot on Sundays" [Back then, Sundays were strictly kept as a Sabbath; even traveling frequently on Sundays was considered breaking the laws of the Sabbath]. Of course, this pastor is on the road a lot on Sundays to visit the ill and those that have been discouraged from church work. However, those who hate him would fabricate a clever lie, deceiving people and raising up complaint, and there is not just one or two of these incidents. (*omitted*) [This has been copied just as printed in *Gil Seon-Ju Moksa Seolgyojib* (*A Collection of Sermons by Reverend Seon-Ju Gil*) by Choi In-Hwa]

There are times when, even though we speak truthfully, we are not careful and thus make great mistakes. A beloved grandson died, so the child's mother comforted the crying grandfather: "Father, please do not cry. I will have another child who is just like this dead child's grandfather." There are people who lead toward the path of life through words, and there are times one leads one down the path of death even with similar words. Once a few years ago, at a time when I was suffering from a deadly heart disease, I heard the words of Joseon women who were visiting sick people, as well as the words of Western women who were visiting. The Joseon people were so worried that they said with great concern and anxiety, "Oh my goodness, that pastor's face has gotten so thin. Your face has become half its size. Oh, look at that face, what are we to do?" When I heard these words, they might as well have said, "You poor man, you are going to die right away." However, the missionaries said to me with a pleasant face, "Ah, Pastor, your face is slowly getting better. Ah, it's better than yesterday." When I heard that, hope rose up in my heart and I felt at peace. So then, when one suffers a sad event, it is easy to make mistakes with words. It is just as easy to make mistakes when going through a joyous occasion. Thus, words can improve a personality but one word can also show the nastiness of that personality. Therefore, I wish for the believers to be models of words.

Conduct

In the old days, a certain teacher took around sixty disciples to evangelize on the streets and they traveled throughout the town. But they did not speak one word of evangelism to anyone and returned. In this way, it was when they did four to five rounds of silent patrol when one person among the disciples asked, "Teacher, what is the reason for going out to evangelize in the streets and not saying one word to evangelize?" The teacher replied, "I have gone around the street a few times, so evangelism has already happened on the street. Let's wait until after this coming Lord's day (Sunday)." The next Sunday, after the teacher gave the sermon he asked if there were any who decided to believe anew, and many said they had been influenced by the teacher's patrol and decided to believe. Let's exude the fragrance of Christ in every place through our actions more than our words. There are many believers who speak well but whose actions are wicked in their family or in normal life.

I hear these words often when I evangelize: "What is it like to believe in Jesus?" When I reply, "If you believe in Jesus you become a righteous person in the world, and you receive the blessings of Heaven after death," they say, "Pastor, stop saying those words. I don't know if ignorant people could believe in the superstition of going to heaven, but stop saying that one can even become a righteous person in this world. Isn't it true that the longer you believe, the more virtuous a person you should be? Those elders and pastors who have believed for decades and have carried out the duties in the church should be befitting men of virtue. However, if you look at those who believe, there are more instances of family discord and fighting in the church. They have jealousy for each other, and they bite and tear each other apart. They have more hot blooded tempers and envy, deception and strife; so do not say that one can become a righteous person in this world." Brothers and sisters! Let us become a light by carrying out a good deed, which witnesses better than talking about it ten times. In any case, let us not be believers who return shame onto Jesus.

Love

The many sayings that insist that nothing is possible without love are written specifically in 1 Corinthians 13. The greatest among the three—faith, hope, and love—is love. It says that "God is love" and also says, "I give to you a new commandment: love one another" (John 13:34), but fighting each other, biting and kicking each other, are evidence of being children of the devil. God's children love their brethren. He who does not love his brethren is a child of the devil, and he who hates his brethren is in darkness, and this dark place is hell. A place without love is hell: a mental hell and a psychological hell are all places without love. All complaints occur because there is no love. The place where there is love is heaven, the earth that has love is paradise, and in heaven love becomes the air itself. If the believers living in heaven have no love, why, I do not want to go to that place. Cain despised his younger brother and killed him, but the Lord commands us to love our enemy. But why do believers despise each other?

A few years ago I was in prison for three years or so, during which time I carefully thought over my thirty years of ministry. Before, I prayed for God to give me the Holy Spirit's power and I indeed received the power and acted upon it as well. Thinking again, I realized the power was for other people and that the power did not improve me. Moses led the Israelites with power, performed miracles and did other extraordinary works, but God did not allow him to enter Canaan, so what good did those miracles and extraordinary works do for him? Though people speak of miracles and extraordinary works that will occur when the Lord returns, they will still be thrown aside by the Lord. There is power in the Lord's name and even though one is not the Lord's disciple one can act in the name of the Lord. Paul had the power to perform miracles and do extraordinary works. But he threw away that authority and desired the love of God, for authority is God's power and love is his strength.

What did I do for several decades? If I went somewhere

and led a revival meeting, that was done by the Holy Spirit's power, not by my own strength. Now I pray this way: "Lord, bestow your loving character upon me. Make me love my family, make me love my brethren, and make me love my church and bestow upon it the character of love." No matter how much learning, abilities, or personality one has, if one does not have love, that learning, ability, and personality would only be for him if he indeed has them—but what good would they be to other people? Rather, he would become arrogant, scorn other people, and would deceive and harm. But there must be love for these to become strength for me, and, at the same time, become something that can save others.

Faith

Faith is the power that wins against the world. Without faith, one cannot please God. The spiritual state of present day believers is empty. For example, when selecting a pastor in the church, many speak of these conditions: Are his associations strong? Is his knowledge abundant? Is he fluent in English? Does he have a good personality? They speak of many conditions but they do not really consider the big question—"Does he have faith?"—as important.

No matter how many sorts of scientific knowledge are

discovered, or how much information is advanced, even if electricity, machinery and all the devices of civilization are invented, one still would not be able to gain salvation through these things. Only by faith can one save their soul. The army often uses means, methods, and skills to be victorious, but the greatest source of their success is faith. Who wouldn't be able to collect that amount of means or methods? The only precious thing is faith, and we must be models of faith.

Holiness

On the billboard of the castle in the heavenly New Jerusalem, it is written, "Nothing impure will ever enter it, nor will anyone who does what is shameful or deceitful, but only those whose names are written in the Lamb's Book of Life" (Revelation 21:27). It says the Father is holy, and Jesus and the Holy Spirit are holy. It is also written, "I am holy, therefore you also be holy" (Jeremiah 11:45). A mother may love her son, but if the child falls into a filthy place and dirties his body and face, doesn't she hug and kiss him only after she has bathed him and washed him clean with water? God loves us but if our hearts are impure and cannot be holy, God will reject us.

I once had a dog in my house. As this dog was very smart,

mild and loved to romp, I loved it immensely. Whenever the dog met me, it would run to welcome me. One day, the dog was on some street eating a young child's feces. When it saw me from afar, it ran bounding toward me. When it tried to get close to me I couldn't allow it at all and kicked it with my foot. It was because his mouth was dirty.

Even though it's true that we love God, if our heart and lips are dirty we cannot escape God's exclusion. Because we are God's children, we must glorify God with a holy lifestyle.

The Three Great Duties of the Believer
2 Timothy 2:15

In these words of encouragement for his young coworker, Paul teaches the three great duties of the believer: the first is presenting oneself as one in whom God delights, the second is becoming the worker who is not ashamed, and the third is discerning the word of truth.

A person's body is made up of trillions of single cells and some seventy odd chemical elements. Each organ of the body has its role, and just as three factors such as pith, energy, and spirit are its main elements [Taoism's three precious elements: They are condensed in the lower, middle, and upper abdomen, and are vital in maintaining life support], there are three great duties for a believer. Even though there are many detailed principles and fine models in all the norms and customs for a life in faith, if one guards these three great duties spoken of here one would gain the essentials. Just as one cannot separate a person's pith, energy, and spirit, one cannot separate these three great duties of the believer and all are duties to be guarded invariably.

The One in Whom God Delights

It is said that this world is "a sea of pain and a valley of tears," but something more tragic than these words can be found in a human life. How did the human world become such a miserable, empty pit? The one who believes in the teachings of the Bible would not hesitate in saying that it is the result of humankind's sin. The sinful life is under the wrath of our Heavenly Father; how then can there be hope or joy? Only destruction and suffering is on that path (Psalm 14).

As an eight-year old, whenever I would study at a private home school and return home, my father would lean on the door and wait for me. When he met me with a big smile on his face and blessed me, nothing could be compared with the joy I felt. But one day I butted a classmate with my head and made his nose bleed. He ran to my house crying and complained to my father about my bad behavior. My father comforted that classmate well and sent him on his way, and he became very angry about my misconduct. I returned home that day, ever so longing for my father's loving face— but what would you expect? My father was furious, and when he glared at me, all my anticipation and happiness changed to fear and despair. I was therefore unable to eat and I stayed up all night in dread. This memory from youth is vivid even now and it serves well as a lesson in faith. How in the world did my hope and joy of yesterday change to great fear and despair? That is because I was happy when my father was happy, but when my father was angry I fell into fear and despair. Before, my father was delighted because of my obedience, but afterwards my father was angry because of my misconduct. In this way our sin has received the wrath of the Heavenly Father.

Even though we try to be happy in our lives through the power of money, wealth adds pain instead; even though people try to be happy through power and influence, power easily causes anger instead; and one covets physical enjoyment but excessive physical pleasure causes self-destruction. Therefore, a wretched world falls even further into a miserable condition.

Believers please God first and then achieve comfort and joy for themselves. Then, how can we make God happy? The greatest is faith, as Paul teaches and witnesses in Hebrews 11:6: "And without faith it is impossible to please God... and he rewards those who earnestly seek him." And he writes to the Philippians proving that even though he is in extreme hardship he is joyful in the Holy Spirit. All these are the joys of faith, and our faith pleases God and will become our sincere joy.

The second is obedience, just as Samuel rebukes King Saul who was disobedient—"Does the Lord delight in burnt offerings and sacrifices as much as in obeying the voice of the Lord?" (1 Samuel 15:22). Believers, if you want to worship, it is imperative that you be obedient first. Rituals do not please God but obedience does.

The third is mercy. God is pleased with mercy but not pleased with sacrifices (Matthew 9:13). How can God be pleased with the worship of one who does not have mercy? Blessed is he who has mercy, for he will also receive mercy. The one who pleases God justly does it through faith, obedience, and mercy.

A Worker Without Shame

In the world there are people who know shame and people who know no shame. The one who knows shame reflects on the sin or faults he has committed in the past and knows how to be ashamed of them; it is easy for this kind of person to repent. As for the shameless person, however, no matter what kind of sin he has committed, he doesn't know how to reflect on it and is just one of the brazen crowd, lacking all sense of shame. It is difficult for this kind of person to repent as the saying goes, "the temperament of an immature and awful person never changes." However, the "unashamed worker" here refers to one who goes into a sanctuary with his head lifted up high because he is a person of faith, and there is no shame in his heart. He has nothing to be ashamed of before God or before humankind.

A person not having anything to be ashamed of refers to their sinlessness. Before Adam and Eve sinned they were in the midst of glory. Even before God they had nothing to be ashamed of, but after sinning once they felt shame before the voice of God, and they could not help but hide among the trees—their concealment in glory having already left them. They couldn't escape the shame of being naked. How can one have jealousy and arrogance in his heart and not be ashamed? Even when one does not lie or slander but does not have a shameful heart, then he is a person who is spiritually dead.

Samuel was a judge of Israel for twenty years, as well as priest, but when he retired from his duties he boldly asked this before God and the people—"Whose ox or donkey have I taken? Whom have I cheated? Whom have I oppressed? From whose hand have I accepted a bribe to make me shut my eyes?" (1 Samuel 12:3). One can point to Samuel and call him a truly "faultless person." The walk of faith and his attitude of evangelism at the end of Paul's life, which

allowed him to confess, "I eagerly expect and hope that I
will in no way be ashamed, but will have sufficient courage
so that now as always Christ will be exalted in my body,
whether by life or death" (Philippians 1:20), was truly
magnificent and beautiful. Thus, Paul was able to urge the
younger generation to be workers without shame. To be a
worker without shame, first, one must serve the Lord with
diligence (Romans 12:11), and second, one must be
faithful (1 Corinthians 4:2).

Discern the Truth

Like the saying, "There will never be a time when
rebellious crowds that put nations in turmoil do not exist,"
in every period were there not deceitful teachers and crowds
who were wolves in sheepskins? Because false prophets
came and went and the incorrect gospel movement
abounded even during the period of the twelve disciples,
Paul had to request discernment of his beloved disciples. If
the need to discern the truth existed even in the first
generation so close to Pentecost, then in modern times,
nearly two thousand years after Pentecost, the necessity of
guarding the truth would be even greater. As I understand it,
what is happening today is the result of the history of
misinterpreted truth and gospel. Heretical movements

always engulf the Lord's sheep and put the church in chaos. Just as counterfeit money closely resembles real currency, and imitation gold looks like pure gold, the words of a false teacher are more beautiful than the words from the lessons of an honest teacher. Therefore, it is easy for the believer to be confused and because the argument of incorrect truths is more rational and in accordance with the times than the faith of the true gospel, it is easy for the church to be confused. Isn't this what the history of the Church shows so well? Sometimes internal chaos erupts. How many times has the church been used by the dark hand of an evil politician, resulting in the merciless spilling of blood? The harms of not discerning the truth are tremendous.

How is the church of the present? There are not many heresies that incorrectly believe that Jesus is only divine. However, there are many believers who worship Jesus merely as a historical figure. Among the people of authority with an instructing position in the church, there are many that possess a dangerously Unitarian faith. Since they do not truly know Jesus, what good could come out of a discussion with them? The meaning of the "Tower of Babel" is "confusion." How great a harm would the Babel of truth cause?

"The persecution of the child born to the woman of the red

dragon" in Revelation 12 speaks of Satan persecuting the church. It would be the most frightening thing to see Satan not only persecuting the church but raising the false teacher as his messenger and confusing the truth. The church being persecuted in this age is represented by the red dragon, namely, one of Satan's works. As a false prophet makes the truth deranged and works harder to break down the faith of the believers, believers and ministers must therefore come to their senses and be alert and awake.

In today's church, it is easy for the truth to be misrepresented under the good name of some project or work. At a certain church, I saw the money that had been gathered at an evangelical meeting being used for night school expenses under the pretense of "Education: One Part of Evangelism." Granted, though education is good, education and evangelism must be regarded as separate things. Although the eradication of illiteracy is an urgent task to be carried out, a night school is a night school and an evangelism meeting is an evangelism meeting. This is a small example, but there are many cases in today's church where people throw themselves into a maze like this. The congregation, elders' assembly or a branch church must always keep in mind what the Lord entrusted and they must guard and dearly hold it in their hearts.

In order to discern the truth, first one must carefully examine the biblical word; second, keep the truth in mind; and third, look over the ideology of this age, stand firm in one's faith, and lead one another so that your fellow believer is not directed toward the wrong path.

Correctly Discern the Grace of the Holy Spirit

A variety of things can appear from the same source: "From a tree that has grown from one root, the flowers are crimson and the leaves are green."

Everyone, look at the beautiful flowers blooming in a garden. There are flowers as white as chrysanthemums, flowers blooming as red as China roses, and among the many flowers that bloom on a spring day are those that are yellow like some blossoms, pure like pear blossoms, and red like peach blossoms, each having its own light. Isn't it strange that the trees and flowers are so different even though they lay their roots in the same soil, receive the same sunlight in the day, and grow in the same wind, the same rain and dew? Does the red flower say to the other flowers, "Flowers are originally red, so white and yellow ones are not flowers"? Flowers are red and pine and bamboo are green, but do the pine and bamboo say to the flower, "Plant life is originally green in color, so red things are not plants"?

Though these plants grow from the same soil, same sun,

and same rain and dew, the fact that their types, colors, and even their names are different is God's providence. Just so, can't we discern the differences of the Spirit's emerging grace according to each person? Inside the church these days, people fail to understand that the Holy Spirit's gifts are different for each person and they end up disputing and fighting. This is what severely darkens one's spiritual knowledge. In a church in North Pyeong'an Province, after it invited a certain pastor for a revival meeting, there broke out a dispute over the split in the congregation between those that shook and those that did not. There was a great scandal with each side arguing that only it had received the Holy Spirit. There are people who shake like the Quakers and people who guard their state so that they do not shake. The disputes do not stop here. There are more than a few disputes rising up in all different regions regarding the appearance of the Holy Spirit. Such disputes have not only occurred in the present. These kinds of problems are evident in every age.

The same Holy Spirit grants different kinds of graces.

Therefore, the apostle Paul teaches in 1 Corinthians 12:4–11, "There are different kinds of gifts, but the same Spirit. There are different kinds of service, but the same

Lord. There are different kinds of acts, but the same God works all of them in all men. Now to each one, the manifestation of the Spirit is given for the common good. To one there is given through the Spirit the message of wisdom, to another the message of knowledge by means of the same Spirit, to another faith by the same Spirit, to another gifts of healing by that one Spirit, to another miraculous powers, to another prophecy, to another the ability to distinguish between different spirits, to another speaking in different kinds of tongues, and still to another the interpretation of tongues. All these are the works of one and the same Spirit, and he gives them to each one, just as he determines." And again alluding to a human body, he teaches this clearly. With this, how will the believer consider precious only the grace you have received and ignore or reject another brother's grace? One Holy Spirit grants different graces to each person in the name of one Lord. Thus brothers and sisters, let us respect one another without being jealous of the grace each and every other person has received.

People are Different and Duties are Different

From the time Samuel was young, he served in the tabernacle at Shiloh; and after he grew up he carried out his duties as a judge and high priest with all his heart as a person in a religious position. However, a wise man like Joseph was not even a high priest or a professional clergyman. With only the position of manager and prime minister, he served the Lord with the lifestyle of a politician. Even so, just as prophets like Elijah and Elisha became images of Christ, Joseph was also a great person of faith who also reflected the image of Christ.

But is Joseph the only one? The great King David was a warrior with blood on his hands. Even so, as a saintly poet, he wrote one-fourth of the poems in the Old Testament, and he praised God for eternity. Praise contributes to two-thirds of a sermon's strength, thus giving him praise with the inspiration of the Holy Spirit is an important work of faith. Also, David was not only a great king of Israel but also a faithful servant of God. So, one can display the Holy Spirit's works of grace even as a warrior and king.

Historically, David's successor Solomon, was a man with unmatched riches as well as wisdom. He flourished so in trade and industry that even just his annual imports of gold reached the enormous amount of 660 talents. He was so wealthy that gold had to replace silver and silver replace bronze. In this way, his glory and honor were immeasurable and reached extremes. Through that wealth he constructed the first temple in Israel and glorified Jehovah God, and as a king of peace he became a reflection of Christ; and with wisdom he wrote the 3,000 proverbs and had the privilege of becoming one of the authors of the Bible.

According to Exodus 31, Oholiab and Bezalel, as mere officials, were inspired by the wisdom of the Holy Spirit and gave glory to God by manufacturing the holy vessel. King Uzziah, as a distinguished politician among the kings of Judah, established irrigation systems and greatly developed agriculture. It would have been fine if he only focused on the politics of promoting agriculture according to the grace he received from God, but he dared to performed the duties of a priest and, as a result, received the punishment of leprosy. As God grants different works of grace and callings to individuals, in the same way, going beyond one's duties not only takes away grace but also results in receiving God's discipline.

Samuel as a priest, Joseph as a politician, David as a warrior and poet, Solomon with wealth and wisdom, Bezalel as a builder, King Uzziah as an agriculturist; each carried out his duties in his own field, but they were all called to God's work by one grace. Just as this, where many shapes of God's grace appear, God's providence is also eternal, and God's glory is infinite. Therefore, as Paul taught through the popular saying during that time in Rome, "If the entire body is an eye, how can it hear, and if the entire body is an ear, how can it smell? For the body is made up of many things but the body is one."

There is No High or Low in God's Works of Grace

Even if one is of low birth, he is still noble if he does his duty to the fullest. Thus, even if one is in the position of a pastor or an elder, he will not be excused of his sin if he cannot fulfill his duties through the Holy Spirit. But even if someone is an unknown believer whom no one knows, he will be able to receive the prize of heaven that is higher than a pastor if he is inspired by the Holy Spirit to live a life of faith and he fulfills the duties of a believer.

As a mere farmer, Judge Gideon was tending the barley fields when he received God's revelation and defeated the powerful army of Midian; when Manoah, the father of Samson, who was called the bravest of the brave, was working in the field, an angel appeared before him from whom he heard the prophecy of Samson's birth; Jacob received God's blessing on the road to Bethel when he was being pursued, and Elisha was plowing with twelve yoke of oxen when he was called by Elijah and received God's commission.

Didn't the above-mentioned people all receive God's

commission as plain farmers of little importance? Who will look down upon someone without position and say that they did not have God's amazing calling and the special grace of the Holy Spirit? We do not need to go far in our analysis: Weren't renowned disciples like Peter, John, and James fishers of the Sea of Galilee? The Holy Spirit's works of grace appear differently regardless of rich and poor, high and low ranks of position, or whether or not one has knowledge.

This much is Christianity's common sense that every believer of today's church assumes to know. But why would an aging person like me suddenly explain this? It is because today's believers, in reality, have the feeling of disregard about discerning the grace of the Holy Spirit—that is why I am revisiting the issue with these words.

As Paul says in Romans 10:8, "The word is near you, even in your mouth, and in your heart," the word is not something far away. Anyone can receive the Holy Spirit's works of grace through faith.

The Responsibility of the Episcopacy—
The 21st Assembly

"Keep watch over yourselves and all the flock of which the Holy Spirit has made you overseers. Be shepherds of the church of God, which he bought with his own blood" (Acts 20:28).

Upon This Occasion

On this 21st Joseon Christian Assembly, I bless the future of the Joseon church and pray for peace to be with all the assembly members. Considering the half-century-long history of the Joseon church, the grace for which I have to give thanks to the Lord is as vast as the heavens, and your services for the sake of the Lord's church, in which you toiled and labored with sincere hearts, will shine for years to come.

However, I do have something to say to the ministers regarding the church's state for the last few years. As it is a bit uncomfortable to address the clergy in a conference where lay believers have also gathered, I waited for the appropriate time to fully express this; however, tonight in this place, where pastors, elders, and missionaries who have important duties in the church have gathered, I step up to the pulpit thinking of how to relay these important words. I ask that you assembly members allow me this opportunity. Also, as I try to speak in this short amount of time, all my sincere thoughts that have been building up in me for a long time, please understand if my words are too intense and out of order or lacking the proper etiquette.

On finishing his three evangelistic journeys, the great apostle Paul, with the resolution of a martyr, requested this of the elders in Ephesus as he bid farewell to them in Miledo, hoping to go back to Jerusalem someday: "Be prudent for your own sake and for the sake of the congregation to raise up God's church." These were Paul's words of final farewell which were also given to the elders of Ephesus; thus, how serious and momentous would it have been? It is not that I address you now boldly with Paul's precise stance and tone, but we who are pastors must also submit to Paul's request. This is, namely, to be prudent for our own sakes, be self-controlled for the followers of Christ, and be discreet for the sake of the Lord's church. These can be called the three cautions of the pastor.

The Higher the Office, the More Important the

Responsibility

Just as Adam and Eve's sins of one moment caused an aftereffect that influenced 6,000 years of all humankind's history, the aftershock of one head pastor's mistake can ruin the entire church. At the time of the First World War, Germany used the tactic of specially targeting enemy officers and assassinating them, causing the Allied side to lose 2,500 generals and commanders and face defeat. When the Allies found out about this, they had all their officers dress in normal soldier's attire and go out to war. In the same way, even the devil uses the tactic of taking down the leaders of the church first. The harm of one pastor's corruption is greater than that of hundreds of new believers.

If we take an example from biblical history, we see that King David did not listen to Joab's counsel and took a census of the people. Because of this deed, all the Israelites were punished with murrain, a plague which targets animals, which killed as many as 70,000 people in three days. If the arrogant sin of one person, King David, killed 70,000 people in this manner, then how many souls destroyed due to a pastor's blunder might there be today?

A few years ago, a young adult believer from South Pyeong'an Province came to visit the church assembly. He watched the congregation, and when he returned, he decided not to attend church anymore. When asked why not, he replied that the sight of the general assembly took away his desire to believe in Jesus. Among lay believers, there are many people who look up to the assembly of elders and the general meeting as a holy gathering. But when they actually witness the meeting, they see that it is not befittingly holy ,and, as a result, they are disappointed. Then how can we not be cautious in our every single word and in our behavior?

But how is the church these days? Though it may not have declined in quantity, I regret to say that its quality is not up to par. Daily, the church is becoming more and more secularized. Since its faith is weak and its love has grown cold, it has lost diligence and power. Gentlemen, how would you look upon today's church? It is more than one or two things that I cannot be optimistic about. There are more than just a few things to worry about.

Why then, is today's church falling into such a state of inactivity and secularization? The clergy that is gathered here today bears that responsibility. Just as one can look at a child and know his father, one can know plenty about the minister by looking at his church. Are believers fighting? This is because that pastor has done so. Are believers loving? Isn't it also because the pastor has been so? One could even say that the believers are a portrait of the pastor.

What Ministers Must be Cautious of

First, today's believers' disrespectful practice of neglecting the Lord's Day is getting more and more serious each day. If you ask why that is so, it is because there are many people among the ministers who do not respectfully keep the Lord's Day. There are pastors who eat out and travel on the Lord's Day; there are many elders who buy and sell goods on the Lord's Day. How will the church keep the Lord's Day holy? Strictly abiding by the rules and regulations decided upon by the elders and congregation while neglecting the Lord's command of keeping the Lord's Day, is reversing our priorities. This is nothing different from the time when the Pharisees regarded human customs as important but thought lightly of the Word of God. One must obey the rules and regulations that come from the Synod; but aren't God's commandments more important? If today's church does not respectfully keep the commandment of the Lord's Day, there is no hope for revival.

Second, neglecting family worship: The family is an altar. But how is it that the sound of praise has ceased from the families of today's church? In many places I have seen families of pastors and elders who do not hold family worship services. With the altar of the family broken down, how is the family complete? With the family incomplete, how can the church be complete?

Third, faults of the mind: A shepherd who is not relying on God's strength and doing things according to his own skills, who is being jealous of one who is a better worker, and who is coveting fame has a wrong mind. The church is most diseased when pastors make these mistakes and commit other negligent faults more frequently than believers. Though the believers pray with diligence, the pastor is lazy in prayer. Though the believers evangelize, the pastor is lazy in evangelism; this is a deplorable occurrence too frequently witnessed.

Fourth, taking pains to acquire a position is a fault that is easy for a pastor to commit. If we are working in the church for the sake of our livelihood, how deplorable would that be? But there were not just a few of these impure, corrupt workers throughout church history; all acts of corruption brewed from them. Even today, are these impure workers not widespread?

When I was released from prison years ago, a certain sister gave me ten *won*, and when asked why, she said it was the money she had saved from fasting one meal a day. I became solemn when I understood the money as the oil of that sister and I gave it to the women's evangelical meeting as an offering. Every single coin we receive from our church members is their oil. But if our pastors only understand church work as a means to employment, how great will that sin of disobedience be? As Ezekiel said earlier, "Because my shepherds did not feed my flock... I am against the shepherds and I will remove them from tending my flock so that the shepherds can no longer feed themselves. I will rescue my flock from their mouths, and it will no longer be food for them" (Ezekiel 34:7–12).

Faith and Love are Above All

My goal is not to try to expose the dark side of the church; nor am I trying to investigate the matter of placing the responsibility for church decline on someone. I am only pointing out that the present situation today is so. I am also wondering how the church of tomorrow may be led properly.

First, feed faith to the believers. For the past decade or so, pastors have surrendered before science and have given up on their faith. They have followed the ways and practices of the world and brought insult upon themselves. They have prioritized business over spirituality and have lost their spiritual power as a result. They ally themselves with the world, and though it seems as if they are welcomed by the world at first, the only end result is that all the church staff, the church believers, and the church are destroyed altogether. Faith comes first; knowledge must come afterward. If the means and ends are correct, there is no reason not to flourish, and reversing the sequence will not leave anyone for survival.

Second, lead the people in love. The late *Boeisa* [*Boeisa* is the Korean name of W. H. Forsythe. Forsythe was a medical missionary, active in the regions of Gwangju and Mokpo], who came to Joseon, gave up his possessions and even his life for Christ and the people of Joseon. He himself was not able to marry, and in the end, he died from an illness. He loved others to such an extent that he cured a certain Joseon woman by sucking out the pus that had formed on her breasts. The teachers of today who consider proper work in accordance with etiquette and honor may criticize him for crossing the line of decency, but love is above decency and honor. Missionary Kipo [Kipo refers to D. L. Gifford, a missionary from the Northern Presbyterian Association] looked compassionately upon a Joseon porter and lent him his horse. The horse, however, ran off with the baggage loaded on its back. That porter looked to Missionary Kipo, cried out resentfully to him, and said, "Since I lost my bags because of your horse, you should pay for my loss." Despite the fact that he had just lost his horse before his eyes, Missionary Kipo paid the porter the value of what was in the bag. A certain missionary who had witnessed this analyzed the incident and claimed there was no reason for him to pay for the goods. However, Missionary Kipo answered, "We must not testify to Jesus with procedure; we must testify to Jesus with love."

If we—including the current ministers and lay believers, those in the presbytery and synod—do our work only by procedure and regulations, we will only become very serious and rigid. If we seek rules on the outside while the inner flesh is ruined, and if we have a firm will without the content of love, then what effect would that have? Without oil a rotary press does not run, and if you try to operate an engine without gas, the machine will only break down. Just as this, a church without love cannot go on. Gas is greater than a machine, and love is greater than rules or specifics. Our presbytery is a core church that includes 300,000 believers and deals with two-thirds of the Joseon church. Therefore, the Presbyterian Church's responsibility for the Joseon church is great. You, the general assembly members—you who spiritually lead the approximately 300,000 believers and almost 1,000 ministers—feed and guide the church in watchful faith and love. But rather, watch over the church for your sake, for the sake of the multitude of believers, and for the sake of the Lord's church.

IV. The Dawn of Peace

Talking Machines and Parrots

One day, I was walking by the house of a foreigner when a plaintive sound of praises came from behind the door. I also heard the sound of many people laughing merrily and talking, and I thought, "What kind of foreigner would be playing merrily like this in this house?" I immediately went in and saw that there was only one person sitting silently in a large room with a machine like a trumpet box [most likely a vinyl record player] in front of him. He had turned it on with his hand and the sound of many people talking was coming out of the box, as well as the sound of plaintive praise and the sound of many people merrily talking. Upon witnessing this I thought, "I was tricked!" and discovered a great meaning that was truly dangerous.

You who toil in only pursuing studies and yet lack fruits for your actions, think about this machine! This is only a machine with chemicals that combine the talking voices on paper called *napbakji* [literally, thin paper made of wax or vinyl]. Once a person's voice is recorded, it will do nothing more than play the person's voice when it is turned on. When you tell that machine to come, it cannot come; and when you tell it to go, it cannot go. Also, an animal called a parrot can copy a person's words as naturally as the flowing of water, but it does not know the meaning of those words, neither can it think on its own. One who believes in the Lord but has not received divine grace only learns academic knowledge and eloquence in speech; he would engage in the art of speaking, give a speech or write an editorial in the newspaper but in actuality he is like a talking machine or a parrot. I once read editorials that certain brothers had published in a newspaper and I listened to another brother's eloquent speaking and speeches. I thought them very precious and truthfully believed them with an open mind but after spending some time with them, I saw that their real actions did not at all match the words they had written in the newspaper or the words they had spoken eloquently. Thus, this was just as if I had been deceived in front of the foreigner's house—listening to sounds coming from the speech machine and thinking it was really the sound of people talking—and it was surely like a person listening to the sound of a parrot and thinking it was a person.

Dear brothers and sisters, what I sincerely want and desire in you is that your actions match the way you speak so that you become true Christians who greatly inspire people's hearts and do not become a talking machine or parrot. Also, you brothers that have received the wisdom of God in managing the church, just as I was deceived by listening to the sound of the talking machine, do not easily make decisions in entrusting important positions to people based merely on the newspaper's editorials, lectures and speeches within the church. I hope that you observe their actions and entrust them with important positions after you see that their words and actions match.

Christ Newspaper February 15, 1906

The Way to Fully Receive the Holy Spirit

There are three stages in receiving the Holy Spirit: the first is receiving the leading of the Holy Spirit, the second is receiving the inspiration of the Holy Spirit, and the third is receiving the filling of the Holy Spirit. Therefore, only after you receive the leading of the Holy Spirit do you receive the inspiration of the Holy Spirit, and after you receive the conviction of the Holy Spirit you receive the filling of the Holy Spirit.

There are six ways to fully receive the Holy Spirit. First, it is by being obedient to God's command. When the Lord ascended to the heavens, the apostles, in being obedient to his command, did not leave Jerusalem.

Second, it is by the unification of the brothers' and sisters' hearts. When the apostles and disciples joined their hearts at Pentecost and gathered in one house, they received the filling of the Holy Spirit like fire in the shape of tongues. If you look at a telegraph wire, the lines must be connected together in order for the electricity to pass through; and so the hearts of brethren must come together for the Holy

Spirit's divinity to come through.

Third, it is through humility. Long ago in the time of the apostles, the centurion of a Caesarean barracks gate was with his family and waiting for Peter to come. When he saw Peter, he went outside the gate and bowed humbly before Peter. With his humble heart, Peter prayed only once and all the people of his household received the filling of the Holy Spirit. The Holy Spirit is like water, and just as much water gathers in a deep place, the filling of the Holy Spirit is received in a person's humble heart. Thus, as the Apostle James says, "God rejects the arrogant and gives grace to the humble" (James 4:6).

Fourth, it is a quiet heart. Thus, when Moses saw God's glory on Mount Sinai and received power, his mind and body silently dwelled in each other. As the Apostle Paul quietly prayed in the Arabian wilderness, he fully received the power of the Holy Spirit.

Fifth, one fully receives the power of the Holy Spirit when he or she toils for the Lord's work. Long ago in the time of the apostles the sorcerer Simon treated the Holy Spirit like an item as he gave money to Peter in seeking the Holy Spirit. However, instead, he was reprimanded. If I foolishly seek to receive the Holy Spirit for my own sake I will instead receive sin. Thus, the apostles and the disciples of the olden days all received the Holy Spirit fully while laboring for the Lord.

Sixth, it is by a sincere prayer. The Lord said, "Ask and it will be given you" (John 16:24). So then, one must not block the leading of the Holy Spirit to receive that guidance. After one receives that guidance, one must not extinguish the inspiration of the Holy Spirit in order to receive that inspiration. After receiving that inspiration, one must first be obedient; second, be united; third, be humble; fourth, be quiet in the mind; fifth, exert oneself in the Lord's work; and sixth, pray sincerely. My beloved brothers and sisters, I hope you ponder over these six methods and work daily to receive the filling of the Holy Spirit.

Christ Newspaper March 8, 1906

The Origin and Meaning of Thanksgiving Day in Joseon

On this day, slightly more than 47 years since our church set down its roots in Joseon, as I introduce the history of Thanksgiving Day—the celebration of the beginning of our church—through your esteemed paper I feel a deep, meaningful joy. Indeed, for me to call this day—a day that changed our lives from being in dark sin to a bright new hope, from death to life, from destruction to establishment—merely "Thanksgiving Day" is somewhat unsatisfying.

The memory of the introduction of Reformed Christianity into our country in 1866, with Mr. Thomas being sacrificed in Pyeongyang along the Daedong River, is still a recent memory for us. After Mr. Thomas, the gospel of Christianity barely and indirectly made its way to us through Southern and Northern Manju [Southern and Northern Manchuria.] However, on September 20, 1884, with the arrival of Mr. and Mrs. Allen, a medical missionary couple from the American Northern Presbytery; the arrival of Mr. Underwood the next year; and doctors Mr. and Mrs. Heron coming to Joseon that same year; our Presbyterian church began to put down its roots in Joseon. Following them, the Fighters of Truth came over and their arrival strengthened the missionaries' vigorous efforts. In the end, they produced the Joseon Christian Presbyterian Assembly.

However in Joseon, because missionaries came over from four denominations, including the American Northern and Southern Presbyterian Assemblies, the Canadian Presbyterian Assembly, and the Australian Presbyterian Assembly, each denomination's missionaries organized a council and led Joseon's early church. While this was going on, believers suddenly rose up in number and three elders, six helpers, and twenty-five missionaries—all of Joseon origin—gathered together and, finally, formed the Joseon Christian Presbyterian Assembly in 1901. They exchanged earnest disclosure of each others' amity and regional situations, as well as intentions for courses of action for the future, and focused on debates; and as young as the church still was, the council that was made up of only missionaries took care of all the work of the actual church.

While doing this, another year passed. The church flourished, and the believers' joy in the life of truth grew daily. When we consider the fact that our church today has achieved this much from the dark Joseon it was, we can only give thanks for God's incomparably ample and great grace. So then, at the 1904 meeting of the Joseon Christian Presbyterian Assembly Council, they decided upon Thanksgiving Day in Joseon with one heart, by the proposal of a member named Elder Seo Gyeong-Jo. And in saying it would be good to enjoy and give thanks for God's grace, they selected five people to be the Thanksgiving Day committee members: Han Wi-Ryeong (Missionary), Weon Du-Wu (Underwood—Missionary), Bang Gi-Jang, Shim Chwi-Myeong, and Ryang Jeon-Baek by the recommendation of President Wang Gil-Ji. They kept the date they had proposed for that year—November 11th on the Julian calendar—as Thanksgiving Day, and each year the council would decide that year's date.

But by the time 1914 came around, the Joseon Christian Presbyterian Assembly had already established itself and the session had become organized. As it was doing all the work on its own, it gathered in Jaeryeong, Hwanghae Province, at the 3rd Joseon Christian Presbyterian Assembly General Assembly; and in the midst of making resolutions on many things, they came to discuss Thanksgiving Day as well. In this, naturally there was much debate concerning the date. The opinion was expressed that it would be better to set the same date for every year, rather than for the general

assembly to decide on a different date each year, and this led
to much discussion about the date. The matter was finally
given over to the Regulation Committee, and what they
decided was subsequently approved in the general assembly.
This is how we are able, even to the present time, to joyfully
celebrate and delight in that day.

But during the discussions that took place at the regulation
board, there were many arguments. There was the idea to
keep the same date as Thanksgiving Day in America. There
was also an idea of selecting our own appropriate date and
celebrating it as Thanksgiving Day now that the Joseon
Christian Presbyterian Assembly was independent. Aside
from these, there were other different opinions but
according to Pastor Underwood's proposal, it was decided
without much dispute that it would be good to make the day
that the first missionary stepped foot into Joseon as the
Joseon Thanksgiving Day.

The first missionaries of the Christian Presbyterian
Assembly to arrive in Joseon were the doctors, Mr. and Mrs.
Allen. Originally, they went to China as missionaries but as
things did not go well according to their wishes they were
encouraged by a certain friend to go to Joseon, and so they
decided to move. Putting in a request to the United States
Northern Presbyterian Assembly Overseas Missions

Department, they were sent as medical missionaries to Joseon. When the Allens' request went to headquarters, the people at headquarters were once again having a discussion about Pastor Underwood's request to move but they had not come to a decision. As a result of Pastor Underwood's determination to work in missions in Joseon and because of his many heartfelt requests to be sent there, MacWilliams, a member of the overseas missions department, donated several thousand *won* for the Joseon mission. And so the entire congregation happily decided to commission Pastor Underwood to Joseon. However, since there was no doctor to help the pastor they were hesitant. Then, when the application to become a Joseon missionary came from Missionary Allen who had been in China, it was immediately accepted and they were commissioned to Joseon. At this time in Joseon, there was an American diplomat named Foote, whose family's lives were greatly threatened in following their own customs because there was no doctor; they couldn't have a stable lifestyle. However, they received news that a doctor was coming. Allen therefore wrote a letter to the diplomat to try and enter Joseon without much trouble and the diplomat publicly announced that Mr. Allen was coming over to Joseon as the doctor at the embassy, arranging it so that there would be no hindrances in Mr.

Allen's landing in Joseon.

He came over to Joseon safely on September 20, 1884. He first learned the language and was preparing the way to proclaim the gospel. Three months had passed since he crossed over to Joseon when finally, a great door opened in order to spread the gospel. Exactly three months after Mr. and Mrs. Allen crossed over, a great political uprising happened which affected all of Joseon but was centered on the Imperial Palace [this refers to the Coup d'Etat in December 1884]. A great disturbance arose in the aristocracy from within the royal court as Min Yeong-Ik—a powerful and influential core political figure, who was a relative of the Empress—was assaulted. It was indeed, this opportunity which God used for opening Joseon. All the famous doctors gathered in Seoul, the capital city and busily tried to save Min Yeong-Ik. Doctor Allen could not stand watching them patching wax on the bleeding sword wound; and with the best methods of medicine he had acquired, he did everything in his power to save Min Yeong-Ik. As a result of his treatments, Min Yeong-Ik's life was restored.

With this event, the country established a national hospital, and, as Mr. Allen was invited as the director, a great path was opened for their purpose of proclaiming the gospel of the Lord Jesus. The gospel that they had brought was not understood in Joseon society at first; people had strange doubts and at the same time did not want to receive the Lord's word which was the gospel of true life. However, through this event, the foundation upon which the kingdom of Christ was to be built was laid in this same society. The following year, many missionaries crossed over with Pastor Underwood and evangelized the people. This destroyed the devil of Joseon and became the seed of the Joseon Christian church in developing a new Joseon.

However, while what was decided in the general assembly was that the date when the first missionaries crossed over to Joseon would be the date of Thanksgiving Day, Mr. Allen's arrival in Joseon was September 20, and Thanksgiving Day is observed on the third day after the third week of November. Therefore, it seems that there was a dispute. But they decided to make it as close as possible to the day the first missionary arrived in Joseon, while also choosing a day after harvest, considering that Joseon is an agricultural society. This is why the day is in a different month from the arrival of the first missionaries. Thus, the third day after the third week of November was decided as the date. In any case, what we must remember is that it is our greatest joy to give thanks for God's infinite grace and to commemorate the day the gospel of grace entered our nation [The table of contents for the Thanksgiving worship service held on November 11, 1931, still survives].

Education of Religion 2. 10 (1931.10)

The Dawn of Peace
John 14:27; Isaiah 32:17; Psalm 85:10

There was a time I received a commission from God and made a voyage on the East Sea. There was also a time I crossed the Hyeonhaetan [Korean pronunciation of Genkai-nada, or the Genkai Sea, off the northwestern coast of the Japanese island of Kyushu] and met a great typhoon. When big waves descended upon the boat from all sides, even though it was a large 5,000-ton ship—I could not describe it as anything else but a leaf—I thought the whole ship was going to drown under those terrifying waves. At that time, I shut the propped window firmly and, going into my bed, could do nothing but feverishly pray that the big waves would become calm, and wait. But the tempest calmed down and as I went up to the deck, what metaphors could I use to describe this? Where did that first storm go? When I saw that it had truly become calm to the point where one could not find a trace of the big waves, what a joy! I truly had joy in my heart and thought if it were as joyful a voyage as this, I would do it several times and still think it was great. When I first witnessed the tempest I thought, "Voyage! Even if I become a Japanese ghost I won't cross the Hyeonhae," but when it had calmed down, I thought, "If the voyage is going to be this joyful then I will always want to go no matter how many times I do it."

But the tempest that hit the continent of Europe did not only shake France for the past four years and four months, but Austria, Russia, Hungary and Serbia as well. They say that from the time the heavens and earth were created there has never been a time when this war, like a great tempest, hit the continent of Europe. The people who have died in the battle and lost their lives after being wounded in Britain, Germany, and Austria are said to be several tens of millions. The wasted money is so much that we cannot count it with our small brains and even when I see such large numbers, it still does not register in my head.

How many millions, or hundreds of millions was it? Or perhaps how many tens of millions, or hundreds of millions was it? In any case I consider the number to be enormous. But this tempest has ceased and is now meeting the dawn of peace; in London; in Paris; the countries that gave the ultimate sacrifice are overcome with their joy. Citizens in France are usually happy and they dance at ordinary times. So when I heard that they were overcome with joy, I was not very surprised. But the citizens in Britain usually remain ever so quiet, speechless, and unexcitable when there is an incident. However, I read an article written in the paper that joy had spread to the point where the British were no less happier than the citizens of Paris. At this, I thought, "That is the way it should be," and I truly sympathized with them. I know that it is the same for you, gentlemen, but from the moment the war started until the Sunday before the armistice treaty was concluded, for four years and several months every morning before God, I tirelessly wished, "Even one day sooner, let this greatest war since creation cease quickly and let peace come quickly, even if superficially." I am sure I was not the only one. I believe several tens of millions of believers of Christ also prayed before God. I remember well Their Majesties the British emperor and empress—of the great sanctuary in Saint Paul, London, who command all the government officials, bowing their heads and praying in that place. However, they were only praying in a disorderly fashion in a thriving place.

However, I know that lowly boys and girls residing at the Andes Mountains or at the foot of the Rocky Mountains, living in a small house that no one would pay particular attention to prayed for this peace. I know there are many people who went down on their knees, clutching the telegram that said their son had died in a battle of this war,

praying, "Even if I have sacrificed like this, God, quickly end
this war by even a day sooner so that other people will not
sacrifice."

One thing aroused my heart very much. The officer of an
American airplane was fighting with a German plane in the
French airspace when the enemy was finally defeated and his
plane went down. The American plane followed behind it
and, as it was gradually descending, he saw that the enemy
had already been killed. So the officer of the American
airplane collected the enemy's corpse, gathered all his fellow
soldiers, and held a fine funeral for him. But from the
moment they started the fight in the air his opponent was
dead. What's more, he carefully wrote about how he had
washed the corpse in order to have the funeral, and relying
on a letter he found in that enemy's pocket that was to be
sent to his hometown, he let the enemy's mother know
everything that had happened. But from the mother came
the reply: "My children have all died. I had only one left but
he has also died. On the dawn of peace, if you please, I would
like for you to visit me. From now on I will love you as my
child." She had received a telegram that said he had killed
the woman's child with weapons but the funeral process was
magnificent, and this German mother did not say one word
of bitter spite but instead greeted him, saying, "You gave him

a fine funeral," and also said, "As I will love you as my son from now on, come visit me at my home." How could the officer of the American plane ever answer this? His answer was not ever recorded and therefore I cannot know for sure, but surely I believe without a doubt that he would have written, "My affectionate mother! *Amo* [Korean for a person's name given to one who is anonymous, like John or Jane Doe]" in the beginning, and at the end, "From your loving son, *Amo*."

But, ladies and gentlemen, I am sure there are plenty of these kinds of tragic stories. The fact that the war has ended and that we now greet the dawn of peace is something that overwhelms me with joy.

This morning we see in Psalm 85:10, "Righteousness and peace kiss each other," and I am sure that many impressions arise from the phrase. In short, has a conflict risen in our hearts that we acted in any way that goes against our real intentions and spoken ill of one another? In truth, in the case that you think you have done an unloving deed to each other, both of your hearts shake just like a wave in the sea. Even when you lie down in bed at night and force down your eyelashes, the fighting in your hearts is fierce and because of it you cannot sleep even if you toss until midnight and the day starts over at one. You think you were so tired when you went to sleep. This time, you dream a dream of being dragged to court and listening to the judge's strict sentence being announced. I know that it is not just one or two times that there has been chaos in your heart. As you wake up in the morning you are so tired that your face is blue and swollen. When people ask, "What is going on? Are you ill?" and not having an illness, you won't be able to say what it is.

Earlier, when I wanted to be a church minister, there was a time when the question of "Have I received salvation?" had surfaced in my heart. For three nights, I could not sleep and I suffered. Until the very end, I could not think of even one time I attempted to betray God. However, there was once when I tried to match God's will but my strength was lacking and I had gone against God's will. If one is a traitor then God punishes, but as the obeying servant of God, I thought of His calling. When I saw that my strength was lacking and how, for the sake of bad habits, I dirtied God's holy name and suffered His holy will even until now, but that He still would not punish me, gradually I came to realize peace in my heart.

Afterwards, there was a time when I saw that I had another great battle to fight in my heart, which embarrassed me a great deal. One person among my close friends was a pastor who was overwrought with the guilt of the sins he had committed. Since he could not go on living this way, he thought of dying, and it is said that he walked to his drawer to grab his razor. However, he was a believer in Christ. He suddenly thought of how Christianity greatly prohibits suicide. He could not even put his hand in the drawer and he left that place. However, he could not live and went back again to die, walking back and forth to the drawer three times. But, he told me, he finally repented, sought the salvation of the cross of Christ Jesus, and received true peace of mind.

However, our hearts receive a great reprimand when something rebukes our true intentions, and when something somehow doesn't allow us to do that which is not appropriate. At that time, there is nothing to do but repent. The sin of the past is something we cannot do anything about. Look to the Lord upon the cross and say, "Father! Forgive me. Redeem me from sin that I will not do unrighteous things like these again," and strangely, in that brief moment, when you sincerely repent, the tempest inside your heart will surely calm, just as a typhoon ceases and the surface of the ocean dies down. You will only be grateful and you will feel nothing but joy as you will come to have a heart like a beautiful spring.

Also, great waves may arise in our families, between the daughter-in-law and her mother-in-law, or perhaps between married couples, which will not die down no matter what. I once saw a daughter-in-law and her husband's mother fighting in the family. The daughter-in-law was the daughter of a nobleman's house, which had authority. As she was the daughter of a nobleman's household, no matter how much she may not have gotten along with her mother-in-law's wishes, there was no reason to send her back to her original family. Therefore, the mother had no choice but to leave her home, which she did one night. The man, who was the husband, went out to find his mother, but no matter how hard he looked he could not find her, and when he could not, he no longer had a desire to live. When he went back out to search for her, he found her and brought her back to the house. The mother returned to the house and was sitting across the wooden verandah when the son took out a dagger to kill himself. A person, who had been standing on the side, took the dagger away and he was not able to achieve his goal. When I heard about the situation and realized that family battles were not to be taken lightly, I could not help but wonder if there was something wicked in the family.

Is your daughter-in-law not good? Is your mother-in-law not good? With whom lies the fault? I think that this is a dynamic fighting scene that concerns all families. Also, the husband only claimed, "The daughter-in-law does not agree with the mother-in-law's wishes." When a man claims his wife loves him only as half her body and he takes another lover somewhere else and does not even come into his house even though she waits for him all night, a wave of enmity rises in that woman's heart. When this wave of enmity rises up, she cannot even express it and she holds it in her little heart … If only she were not in this world, then things would be better. Therefore, she thinks several times: "Should I hang myself?" "Shall I stab myself with a dagger?" or even, "Should I throw my body into the sea?" And when those kinds of waves of enmity rise up, the pain of her suffering cannot be expressed in words. In this kind of situation, what should be done? If the husband were to have "righteousness and peace kiss each other" then there would be nothing for him to do besides getting rid of that lover. If he were a believer there would be nothing for him to do but pray feverishly, "Father! Get rid of that other mistress for me," and entrust it to God. If he thought of it as commonplace and hoped to be rid of it somehow, then peace would never come into that family. If the woman cannot allow this to go on any longer and begins to fight for the sake of the children's education, for the sake of the evangelism of the family, and for the sake of her husband; if she holds that heart of righteousness firmly even if she is kicked or punched, she would win the battle in the end and peace would come upon that household: "Righteousness and peace would kiss." What could be more joyful than the beauty of when that righteousness and peace kissed between heaven and earth? I know there would be no time as joyful as then.

Facing a vague situation is like spreading a mat on top of what is arising to cover it and never knowing when it will explode. On the surface it seems like a cushion good for sitting, but it pierces underneath. In any case, one must extract that piercing object and throw it away so that there is absolutely nothing piercing at the bottom even if it means standing there or dancing on top of it. Only then will righteousness and peace kiss one another.

In the case of this war, my friends, you must remember this: The Austrian Crown Prince was assassinated by a young man called Gavrilo Princip of Serbia on June 28, 1914. Not only was the Austrian Crown Prince struck but Her Royal Highness was as well. Afterwards, a great conflict arose but the assassination of that Austrian Crown Prince and Her Royal Highness was forgotten after a while because Germany soon penetrated Belgium, a country which was a perpetually neutral zone, and attacked France. Britain raised the banner because it realized that Germany must be struck. It was thought that the hundred million citizens of America that had advocated justice and humanity during the time of peace would support Britain's attempt at righteousness, but instead America was quiet and unwilling to help. It seemed that America was all talk; they said they could not become an opponent. Even though this went on for two years and a few months, America did not want to stand up. Only when a German submarine attacked and sank the Lusitania, an American merchant vessel, did America become one to say it would not rest until Germany was hit, which was the beginning of April 1917 [This ship was attacked on off the coast of Ireland by a German submarine during the First World War on May 7, 1915. Out of the 1198 people that perished, 128 were American; this escalated the conflict between Germany and America, and became the reason America entered the war in April of 1917].

Why couldn't President Wilson stand up from the beginning, when he had made that speech about 'justice'? As you know, among America's 100 million people, 30 million are of German origin. If America combined its strength with Britain and France and came to attack Germany, then the majority of those 30 million would have to rise up from the inside. Thus, America had to be patient and wait for as long as it could. In any case, they resisted participating until even the majority of the 30 million Germans in America also agreed that Germany was immoral. However, when Lusitania was attacked, Wilson cried out. America agreed, as one, and rose up when the time came that they had no choice but to rise up. Thus, Britain and France gained power and claimed a great victory, as the shame of the people was taken away. But America only had around 100,000 casualties from the war. Even so, because America stood up, the Allied Nations was able to claim victory this time. It is true that they stood up with the idea of morality and justice in mind as they thought, "If we do not hit Germany, it will not be fair." It was not that America sought territory in Europe, as if it wanted some kind of continental territory in Europe for their country's branch office. In any case, with the thought that they must strike Germany and its immorality, they stood up.

Finally, within a few days we met the dawn of peace, the peace treaty conferences began. How did that peace conference go? The peace meetings were supposed to go on until today, but how did they end? Britain has used such prestigious words of "peace conference of justice," but what of the fact that it has expanded its territory to a point that they say, "There is no place in the world where the sun does not set on British territory?" Is it not deliberately stealing another's country? They have stolen to greatly expand their country, but only in this battle do they cry out for justice. Of course, it is true that Britain has stolen others' land on the one hand. When it steals others' land, it did not fight the battle of justice—this may be so. However, even in Britain, the mind of its people and its public opinion changed from the end of the nineteenth century until the beginning of the twentieth century, so that people thought a country must be founded on justice, and this thought progressed. America also came to the same conclusion with Britain. From the time the fighting began until now, America has said, "What fools, those British!" and did not share the same mindset with them, but even America unified with Britain because it saw that Britain's method was extremely fair and just; it said, "If it is for the sakes of justice and humanity, then we will help," and sent troops and lent them money.

When we reflect on America's conclusion to "being together no matter what," we see that Britain's notion of justice has been approved by America. Americans, as you can see in the fighting of their Civil War between the North and South, fight for the sake of justice and humanity. This, therefore, was something for which they could not but fight. The fact that this was for the sake of justice and humanity is something that one can agree with, if one is a person who knows America, namely a person who lives on American soil. Then, at the start of this peace conference, would people who speak well like Sojin [A powerful political figure in the time of China's civil wars] and Jangui [A politician of the Wi Dynasty during the time of civil wars in China] gather to expand their territorial land?

I cannot believe it. People like Lloyd George, Clemenceau, and Wilson did not really talk about these international situations when they consulted with each other. However, I am sure decisions were made when they intimately talked with each other. But even if General F. Foch or General Hyeok were to join, I am certain that the meeting would have progressed as if intimate friends who have always worked and talked together, had gathered to decide on the outcome of the events. Moreover, plenipotentiary ambassadors came from China and even while other plenipotentiary ambassadors of other countries ....

....

....

....

.... [This part of Reverend Gil Seon-Ju's sermon was deleted after inspection by the Japanese government. Reverend Gil Seon-Ju was one of the important political figures who signed the Independence Declaration for the March 1st Movement, and even experienced hardships as a result. The fact that parts of this sermon have been cut shows Reverend Gil Seon-Ju was not only a minister but a national leader].

When will the words, sung by a poet before Jesus' time, of peace and righteousness kissing each other come true? Or when will Jesus' proclamation of peace on the cross be realized? We will have to wait and see. I did not think that the peace conference held after World War I would be like the peace conference of deceit in Hague just twenty years before. I did not think these talks, too, would be brought to an end by cunning means but that they would continue on the basis of justice, heart to heart, mind to mind. But how did it end? World peace, it seems, does not exist for the weak. Ladies and gentlemen, do not let your heart be swayed, and from today on you must remember the words, "Peace kisses righteousness." One that fights on the foundation of justice would pray "open your hands from above and rule" so that the curtain of peace will open on the stage of righteousness. However, if we as individuals do not repent after committing sins, peace would not come into our hearts. Even when there is fighting in the family and it seems like we have chased the unrighteous person out because it did not seem that the righteous one could win, true peace will not come into the family. The reason there are fights between nations is because either side is unrighteous. If the world relies on justice and humanity but then does not behave that way, I do not think peace will come hereafter. But either way, I say it again: I sincerely hope and wish that you pray before God and seek him through these words in Psalm 85:10, "Righteousness and peace kiss each other."

A Collection of Sermons from Distinguished Religious
Leaders (1921)

* This sermon is included in the collection of sermons called *A
Collection of Sermons from Distinguished Religious Leaders*, the
Korean Protestant Church's very first collection of sermons published
in July of 1921. This collection, published after the March 1st
Movement, shows the development of the Korean church in the early
twentieth century and the need for a cultural movement. This sermon
by Gil Seon-Ju, titled "the Dawn of Peace," borrowed its form from that
of the cultural movement, and a part of it was detected and deleted by
the government as a result. In this way, this sermon shows the passion
for peace and interests in social issues of Reverend Gil Seon-Ju, who
was one of the important figures who signed the declaration of
independence for the March 1st Movement and experienced hardships
as a result

Praise for Elder Ju

1. Tonight in the city of David
   Christ is born.
   Like the shepherds of Bethlehem's fields
   We go quickly in search of the Lord.

2. The heavenly messengers proclaim—
   They praise with the celestial army.
   As the wise men of the east rejoice,
   Let us also rejoice!

3. The wise men of the east see the star,
   And rejoice the most joyfully—
   They worship before the baby
   And offer gifts they have prepared.

(Chorus) How joyful and joyful
Jesus the Savior is born.
From the time when heaven and earth were created
So as to make life.

He became a glory to God.

Joy to the people of the world!

Among many joyous days

The greatest is the day the Lord was born.

How joyful and joyful!

Jesus the Savior is born

Christ Newspaper February 15, 1906

* This hymn was composed by Reverend Gil Seon-Ju, who wrote the poem while lamenting the fact that Elder Ju Gong-Sam, ministering in Namdo (Southern Provinces) at the time, could not spend Christmas with him. This short poem of praise shows Reverend Gil Seon-Ju's literary fluency; he was also proficient in poetry and writings of unrhymed verse.

A Pulpit Handbook: Jesus's Seven Footsteps
1 Peter 2:21

Preface

The Lord said, "I am the way, the truth, and the life. No one comes to the Father except through me," so without following the Lord's footsteps, one may never enter heaven.

I. Traces of descent

1. Traces coming down from heaven to earth (Matthew 1:23)

2. Traces residing on the lowly earth (Matthew 2:23)

3. Traces of a servant (Philppians 2:6–7; Matthew 20:28)

II. Traces of prudence

1. When tested on tax issues in Rome (Matthew 22:21)

2. Concerning the temple tax (Matthew 17:27)

3. When tested by the lewd woman (John 8:6–11)

III. Traces of weariness

1. Traces of hunger and thirst (John 4:6–7)

2. Traces of being exhausted (Matthew 8:24)

IV. Traces of determination

1. Traces of winning over the Devil's test (Matthew 4:1–11)

2. Traces of not shaking in people's tests (John 6:15)

3. Traces of not being pulled by recognition (John 2:24–25)

V. Traces of brave advances

1. Traces of brave advances in times of peace (Matthew 4:23–25)

2. Traces of brave advances in times of peril (John 18:4–8, 11:8; 19:39–41)

VI. Traces of grief

1. Traces of grief for disciples (John 11:35)

2. Traces of grief for the world (Luke 13:34–35)

3. Traces of grief for himself (Matthew 26:37–38)

VII. Traces of hardship

1. When he was born (Luke 2:7)

2. When he evangelized (Matthew 8:20)

3. When on the road (Luke 9:51–56)

4. On the cross (Luke 22:44; 23:39)

Conclusion

When we follow the footsteps of the Lord, we will receive the crown.

A Pulpit Handbook (1926)

* Reverend Gil Seon-Ju's *A Pulpit Handbook* is a collection of summaries of sermons, with more than 200 sermons and their outline. This book provided a model of sermon outlines for ministers in the Korean church. One such outline is included here so that the readers may see Reverend Gil Scon-Ju's sermon outline on their own. This book was originally published in January of 1926 and re-published in 1958 under the title of An *Example from Reverend Gil Seon-Ju's Sermons: A Pulpit Handbook*. For the reader's convenience, the editor has re-written the outlines based on Lee Seong-Ho's edited version published in 1969, while primarily relying on the original copy of 1926.

A Biblical Commentary on Daniel

Introduction

I. Daniel was of a royal family in the line of Judah.

II. It was the 3rd year of Jehoiakim King of Judah, when he became a captive—eight years before Ezekiel was taken as a captive. It was during the time of B.C. 606–605, when he was about 16 years old.

III. The place he studied was the palace of the foreign monarch, King Nebuchadnezzar.

IV. He received three great temptations.

1. At the destruction of the kingdom of Israel

2. At being taken captive

3. At becoming a eunuch (2 Kings 20:18; Isaiah 39:7)

V. He led three kings in times of trouble.

1. King Nebuchadnezzar (Daniel 4:1; 3:37)

2. King Darius (Daniel 6:26–27)

3. King Cyrus (Ezra 1:1–2)

VI. The Book of Daniel was written between B.C. 605 and 530.

VII. The content of the book resembles the New Testament's Book of Revelation.

1. Exiled (banished)

2. Receives revelation

3. Purified

4. Becomes a member of royalty

<Outline> The Book of Daniel can be divided largely into two parts.

I. The first section, chapters 1–6, is a chronicle.

II. The second section, chapters 7–12, is a prophecy.

Chapter 1—Daniel's ordeal (taken as captive)

I. Daniel suffers (1:1–7)

1. Loses the inscription of the temple in the kingdom of Israel (1–2)

2. Becomes a eunuch (3)

3. Endures shame (4)

4. Forced to eat food that is unclean (5–7)

5. Given new names

    (1) Daniel named Belteshazzar

    (2) Hananiah named Shadrach

    (3) Mishael named Meshach

    (4) Azariah named Abednego

II. Tested (1:8–16)

1. Determined to pass the test (8)

2. Receives God's grace (9)

3. Passes the test (10–16)

III. Receives the prize (17–21)

1. Masters education (17)

2. Receives great authority (18–19)

3. Excels in wisdom (20)

4. Lives long in this world (21–)

Chapter 2—King Nebuchadnezzar's dream of a giant statue

I. Scholars are unable to understand the king's dream (1–13)

II. Daniel prays for wisdom (4–18)

III. Daniel receives revelation (19–30)

IV. Announces King Nebuchadnezzar's forgotten dream (31–35)

V. Interprets the dream for him (35–45)

1. Gold as Babylon

2. Silver as Persia

3. Bronze as Greece

4. Iron as Rome

VI. Daniel is exalted (46–49) and appointed to a high office

Chapter 3—Nebuchadnezzar's pride

I. Nebuchadnezzar erects a golden idol (1–7)

II. Daniel's three friends do not bow down to the gold statue
(8–18)

IV. Daniel is thrown into the lion's den (16–17)

V. God protects and saves Daniel (18–24)

VI. Darius lays down a new royal edict (25–28)

Chapter 7—Daniel's vision of the beasts

I. Introductory words (1–3)

II. Sees four beasts (4–8)

1. Lion—Babylon (4)

2. Bear—Medes and Persia (5)

3. Leopard—Greece (6)

4. The terrifying and frightening beast—Rome (7)

5. The little horn—the anti-Christ (8)

III. The Lord of Judgment appears (9–28)

1. God is seated (9–14)

2. The Savior of the New Testament appears (13–14)

3. Interpretation of the revelation (15–28)

Chapter 8—Revelation of the Ram and Goat

I. Revelation (Revelation 1–14)

1. The time of revelation (1)

2. The place of revelation (2)

3. The ram (3–4)

4. The goat (5–8)

5. The little horn (9–12)

I. Events of Medes, Persia, and the Kings (1–2)

II. The achievements of the kings of Greece (3–20)

III. The achievements of Antiochus and Epiphanus (36–45)

Chapter 12—The mystery of the last days

I. Great suffering (1–)

II. Resurrection (2–3)

1. The first resurrection

2. The second resurrection

III. Daniel hears the secret conversation of angels (4–10)

IV. Numbers of the last days (11–13)

Gangdaebogam and A Biblical Commentary on Daniel (1969)

* Reverend Gil Seon-Ju's *A Biblical Commentary on Daniel* is a text that contains an outline of Daniel for those that wish to lecture on Daniel. Just as it can be seen in *A Study of the End Times* and *The Attinment of All things*, he had a special interest in the Last Days. In this way, *A Biblical Commentary on Daniel* shows Reverend Gil Seon-Ju's interest on the Last Days, as well as a model for sermon outlines.

Suggested Readings for Reverend Gil Seon-Ju

I. Primary Original Sources

Gil Seon-Ju, *Haetaron* (*Sloth*) (The Bible Society of Korea, 1904).

  * This book is a reworked, shortened version of John Bunyan's *The Pilgrim's Progress* for evangelism and education. The original script is 20 pages long. An English translation and a brief introductory summary is in the first issue of *KIATS Theological Journal*: (2005, 86–95)

Gil Seon-Ju, *Mansa Seongchwi* (*The Attainment of All Things*) (Gwangmun, 1916).

  * This is a reworked version of John Bunyun's *The Pilgrim's Progress*, incorporating illustrations and Chinese poetry. The original script is 59 pages long. KIATS is planning to publish it in both English and modern Korean.

Gil Jin-Gyeong, *Selected Posthumous Writings of Rev. Young'gye Gil Seon-Ju, Vol. 1.*

  * This book was edited by Rev. Gil Jin-Gyeong as a collection of Rev. Gil Seon-Ju's posthumous work. This book includes valuable sources such as *A Study of the End Times*, "A History of Pyeongyang Sanjeonghyeon Church," and "A Historical Record of Pyeongyang United Women's Association ."

Lee Seong-Ho, ed. *Korean Writings of Faith Vol. 1: Rev. Gil Seon-Ju's Sermons and an Abridged Edition of His Complete Works* (Seoul: Hyemun, 1969).

* This book contains a collection of Rev. Gil Seon-Ju's sermons as well as a biography written by Rev. Kim In-Seo, originally published in *Sinhakjinam*.

Lee Seong Ho, ed. *Korean Writings of Faith Vol. 2: A Pulpit Handbook and A Biblical Commentary on Danie*l (Seoul: Hyemun, 1969).

* This book contains summaries of Rev. Gil Seon-Ju's sermons, including *A Pulpit Handbook* and *A Biblical Commentary on Daniel.*

Choi, In-Wha, ed. *Gil Seon-Ju Sermon Collection* (Gyeongseong: Jugyo, 1941).

* This book contains Gil Seon-Ju's 19 sermons and 28 sermon notes. This publication is regarded as the most credible among Gil Seon-Ju's sermon collections.

** Other important transcriptions include *A Song of the Gentleman's Springtime Dream amid the Mountains and Trees, History of Gil Yeong'gye,* and *Gil Seon-Ju's Parable Collection.* These transcriptions are collections of the Library of Presbyterian College and Theological Seminary in Korea.

2. Secondary Materials

(1) Texts

Gil Jin-Gyeong, *Yeong'gye Gil Seon-Ju* (Seoul: Jongro, 1980).

* Rev. Gil Jin-Gyeong, the second son of Rev. Gil Seon-Ju, published his father's autobiography after 20 years of planning. This is the definitive edition of studies on Gil Seon-Ju; this autobiography divides his life into five periods and reports on it based on numerous domestic and international sources. Samuel Moffet's preface and 8 chapters of appendix present additional rare sources.

Gil Jin-Gyeong, *A Collection of Rev. Gil Seon-Ju's Illustrations* (Seoul: Christian Literature).

* This book contains illustrations, proverbs, and summaries of sermons that Gil Seon-Ju has left behind. Gil Jin-Gyeong, the second son of Gil Seon-Ju, edited this book, and Gil Hwa-Yeong, granddaughter of Gil Seon-Ju, published it.

(2) Articles

Kim Seok-Hwan, "Rev. Gil Seon-Ju and the Korean Church," *Calvin Forum* 24 (2004): 311—332.

Kim Seung-Cheol, "The Relationship between the March 1st Independence Movement and the Revivalist Gil Seon-Ju."

Mok'won University Theses Collection 47 (2006): 79–90.

Na Dong-Kwang, "Gil Seon-Ju's Life and the Nationalistic Movement," *A Collection of Theses on Culture and Tradition* 9 (2001): 117–129.

Mun Baek-Ran, "A Study of Gil Seon-Ju's Eschatology," *Church and History* 4 (2000): 62–79.

Ok Seong-Deuk, "The Great Revival Movement in Pyeongyang and the Taoistic Influence of Gil Seon-Ju's Spirituality," *Korean Christianity and History* 25 (2006): 57–95.

Lee, In-Jae, "A Study on the Revival Movement of the Korean Church: Gil Seon-Ju, Kim Ik-Du, and Lee Yong-Do as Central Figures," *Korean Theology* 27 (2005): 136–160.

Lee, Hyeon-Woong, "Gil Seon-Ju, The Leader of the 1907 Pyeongyang Revival Movement: His Life and Sermons," *Theological Thought* 137 (2007): 289–325.

Heo Ho-Ik, "The Characteristics of Korean Theology in Rev. Gil Seon-Ju's Eschatology," *Theology and Culture* 16 (2007): 297–323.

(3) Theses in English

Kim In-Soo, "Protestants and the Formation of Modern Korean Nationalism, 1885–1920: A Study of the Contributions of Horace Grant Underwood and Sun Chu Kil," Union

Theological Seminary in Virginia, Ph.D. Thesis, 1993.

Kim Shin, "Study of the Contributions of Sun Joo Kil to the Formation of the Presbyterian Church in Korea," Fuller Theological Seminary, M.A. Thesis, 2001.

Chronology of Pastor Gil Seon-Ju

Mar 15, 1869 – Born in Hujang-dong, Anju,
South Pyeong'an Province.

1889–1896 – Devotes himself to the training of *Seon*,
including *Kwanseong-gyo*.

1897 – Baptized at Neoldari Church.

1898 – Appointed as a lay leader of Jangdaehyeon Church.

1903 – Enrolls at the Pyeongyang Presbyterian
Theological Seminary.

1904 – Publishes *Haetaron* (*Sloth*).

1906 – Begins the first early morning prayer meetings in Korea.

1907 – Graduates as a member of the first class
from Pyeongyang Presbyterian Theological Seminary.
Appointed as pastor of Jangdaehyeon Church.

1916 – Publishes *Mansa Seongchwi*
(*The Attainment of All Things*).

1919 – Signs his name on the Declaration of Independence
as one of the 33 national representatives
of the March 1st Movement.

1926 – Publishes *Gangdae Bogam* (*A Pulpit Handbook*).

Nov 26, 1935 – Passes away while leading a revival Bible class
in South Pyeongyan Province.

Translator: Hannah Kim

Hannah Kim is the daughter of a pastor, raised in the United States. She has worked and studied in Korea and currently resides in Los Angeles, California.